CW01018890

# THE BEACHMAN'S COAST SUFFOLK

## Coastal Communities and their Boats

─────ROBERT  SIMPER─────

# THE BEACHMAN'S COAST SUFFOLK

## Coastal Communities and their Boats

### Vol 5 The Coast in the Past Series
### ROBERT SIMPER

Published by Creekside Publishing 2015.
www.creeksidepublishing.co.uk
ISBN 978-0-9563299-4-3

*Front cover* Noel Cattermole and Peter Runnacles hauling the *Joseph William* off Sizewell beach using a power capstan with a rope attached to an anchor, 2014. *Back cover* The *Shady Nook* on Thorpeness beach.

Printed by Lavenham Press Ltd, Lavenham, Suffolk.

Books by the same author

## EAST ANGLIAN BOOKS
*Over Snape Bridge* (1967)
*Woodbridge & Beyond* (1972)
*Suffolk Show* (1981)
*East Anglian Coast & Waterways* (1985)
*Suffolk Sandlings* (1986)
*Woodbridge: Pictorial History* (1995)
*Suffolk: A Fine Farming County* (2007)
*Woodbridge to the Coast* (2008)
*Coastal Suffolk* (2009)
*Coastal Essex* (2011)

## SAIL BOOKS
*East Coast Sail* (1972)
*Scottish Sail* (1974)
*North East Sail* (1975)
*Victorian & Edwardian Yachting from Old Photographs* (1978)
*Gaff Sail* (1979)
*Sail on the Orwell* (1982)
*Sail: The Surviving Tradition* (1984)
*The Cambria Story* (2012)

## BRITISH ISLES
*British Sail* (1977)
*Britain's Maritime Heritage* (1982)
*Beach Boats of Britain* (1984)

## ENGLISH ESTUARIES SERIES
*The River Deben* (1992)
*The River Orwell and the River Stour* (1993)
*Rivers Alde, Ore and Blyth* (1994)
*Essex Rivers and Creeks* (1995)
*Norfolk Rivers and Harbours* (1996)
*Thames Tideway* (1997)
*River Medway and The Swale* (1998)
*Rivers to the Fens* (2000)
*Up the River Deben* (2006)

## AUTOBIOGRAPHICAL
*In Search of Sail* (1998)
*Family Fields* (1999)
*Voyage Around East Anglia* (2001)
*Creekside Tales* (2004)
*The Best Crop* (2013)

## COAST IN THE PAST SERIES
*Forgotten Coast* (2002) British Isles
*Sunrise Coast* (2002) Suffolk & N.Essex
*The Lugger Coast* (2003) Cornwall & Devon
*The Barge Coast of Suffolk, Essex and Kent* (2007)

# CONTENTS

# BACKGROUND TO THE RESTLESS COAST

The slow and painful decline of the North Sea fishery from Lowestoft has been very well recorded, but no one seems to have taken much notice of a similar decline in the boats working off the open beaches. I have attempted to redress the balance and tell the story of the Suffolk beachmen. The state of the beaches is an important part of this story.

The Suffolk people have a heroic record for trying to save their restless coast and, at the same time, make the best use of the coast as a place to live and work. The North Sea has never been kind to the Suffolk coast, and continues to batter it endlessly. The coast has changed shape and receded so that the beaches that the Anglo-Saxons and Vikings walked on are now far out to sea.

The coast that early medieval people knew must have been totally different. The eroding sand and shingle has blocked up several small estuaries. As the numerous estuaries were closed the longshore fishermen were forced to work their boats off open beaches. To do this they evolved boats suitable for landing on exposed beaches.

Whole communities grew up working boats off open beaches, not just fishing, but for salvage, pilotage and summer pleasure trips. All the beach boat activities reached a peak in about 1895 when there would have been over a thousand families dependant on the beach boats for a living.

Anyone making a passage along the Suffolk coast early in the twentieth century would have seen large fleets of lug-rigged boats at work. By the end of the twentieth century the number of fishing boats was falling, but fishermen still had to keep a careful watch for boats crossing their bows on the way back to the beaches.

When I was young, just after World War II, beach boats used for salvage and pilotage had already gone, but there were still many boats fishing and others running summer trips for visitors. In 1984, when I wrote 'Beach Boats of Britain,' some beach landings were already empty, but commercial fishing had become centralised on Aldeburgh beach. With about twenty-four wooden boats, Aldeburgh beach had the largest beach landing fleet in East Anglia and appeared to have a long-term future.

Fishermen are primarily interested in catching and selling fish and their boats are just tools they use to achieve this end. However longshore fishermen can't make a living without the knowledge of the seabed and the seasonal habits of the fish. In the past young men watched where the older men were fishing, but that chain of knowledge was lost as the older men gave up.

Fishermen changed their boats to adapt to new forms of fishing and many open Suffolk boats are left dotted around the East Coast estuaries. Most people just think of them as being motor launches and they often finish up being used for lifting moorings or as pleasure boats. Very few people recognize them as a type of local traditional workboat that could virtually float on a heavy dew, but ride on the seas like a duck.

In 1981 my son Jonathan found the rotting hull of the beach boat *Three Sisters* in Ralph Brinkley's boatyard at Orford. I realised that she was one of the few sailing hulls left and we had her rebuilt. She turned out to be a very practical boat for day trips under sail or motor and we have visited many places between Maldon and Lowestoft.

Thirty-two years later we bought the *Our Boys*, another beach boat damaged while being used to lift moorings and lying in exactly the same place in the Orford Boatyard. She has been brought up to standard and re-registered as a fishing boat so that my grandson Harry Simper can work her longlining and in our shellfish business. We have collected a small fleet of boats built to work off the Suffolk beaches; the *Three Sisters (1896)*, *Pet (1922)*, *Shady Nook (1955)*, *CK ex-Douglas (1975)* and *Our Boys (1976)*.

While our wooden boats may be out-dated, the coast's problems with flooding and erosion remain the same. In the nineteenth century there appear to have been nine very high tides, causing flooding and large-scale damage to the coastal area. The landowners and town councils took this damage very seriously and began strengthening sea defences. There was serious flooding with a big tide in 1906 and after World War II the government took on the role of defending the nation against flooding. Sadly they were not in time to defend the coastal community against the 1953 tidal surge. After this, Government massively increased sea defences, but gradually people began to forget about the serious flooding and resources were diverted elsewhere. Fortunately the defences were in reasonable order so that when the St Jude's Day Flood of December 2013 swept the coast no one was drowned-a major achievement-although many properties were flooded. All the Government expenses over the

previous decades were justified in one night.

In Britain there has always been a knee jerk reaction to flooding and erosion, then it gets forgotten. After the December 2013 flooding money was suddenly available to put right some of the damage. Across the North Sea our neighbours have exactly the same problems, but there is no erosion in Belgium or The Netherlands, because they plan forward and think out a strategy to protect the whole coast

On the Suffolk beaches there is no hint of the political struggles that go on to defend the coast against the powerful force of the sea. The shingle crunches under your feet while the sound of the waves crashing on the shore rings in your ears and actually give a great sense of freedom. It is a place to let your problems blow away in the salt laden air.

Simpers of Suffolk; *Our Boys* returning from longlining past Felixstowe Ferry. 2014.

# ACKNOWLEDGEMENTS

Most of the information here naturally comes from the fishermen and boat builders. Some of people who supplied information are no longer with us, such as Henry Beeton and Billy Bere who used to talk a lot about their early days around Shingle Street. Harry Harling and Percy Westrup enjoyed reminiscing about their fishing days at Thorpeness. At Kessingland, 'Cock Robin' Brown and Roy Brown also enjoyed talking about the old days.

Starting at the southern end of the coast I was helped with information on Bawdsey by Vic Clouting and his daughter Diana Clouting, while across the river at Felixstowe Ferry, John White helped with boat building information, and Tam Grundy talked about fishing in the *Moonraker*. Material on Shingle Street came from Sarah Margittai, Alex Burwood, Elizabeth Maskell, Philip Maskell, Graham Hussey and Bruce and Anne Page. Nicholas Gold arranged for Pete Benstead to take us out to Orfordness. At Aldeburgh, Richard Burrell, Richard Marson, Nicholas Hill, Ann Krejsa and Margaret Ballard have refreshed my knowledge of Aldeburgh beach, while Bryan Upson talked about boats built in his boatyard at Slaughden.

John Westrup, Tony Ralph and Russell Middleditch kindly gave information about the final years of fishing off Thorpeness beach. Also John lent his uncle Percy Westrup's written account of fishing that started in the late Victorian period. David Cleveland made me aware of the boatbuilding at Leiston while Noel Cattermole was a fund of information about Sizewell. On the Dunwich boats Stephen King also was a mine of information. At Southwold John Winter, John Goldsmith and Laurence Vulliamy supplied material and the Southwold Museum photographs. Jane Hart has kindly lent photographs that her uncle Edward Hunter took at Kessingland in the 1930s. Edward Hunter had a shop in the village and used to supply photographs and stories to the 'News Chronicle' which often meant a dash to get to Lowestoft to put them on the train for London. John Yeardley filled me in on the Lowestoft fish trade.

The artists Mark Myers, James Dodds, Roger Finch, Janet Harker and Ruth Ufford have brightened up this book with their work. Another artist, Claudia Myatt, created the wonderful coastal map and helped with the editing.

Tracking the origins of photographs is always difficult, particularly now, in a digital age, when there is no way of tracing the original photographers. The East Lane, Bawdsey postcards are owned by Liz Marks and were lent by Diana Clouting. Robert Moore Ede supplied the photographs of the 'Jolly Sailor' at Orford. Some Southwold photographs came from John Cragie and Southwold Museum.

My son Jonathan Simper and grandson Harry have been very helpful about the beach boat era. This project would not have been possible without the invaluable help from my wife Pearl. She took some of the colour photographs while I have taken most of the others.

**RS. Ramsholt, 2015.**

The Newson's pleasure boats *Orwell Viking* and *Deben Viking* at their landing stage on Undercliff beach, Felixstowe in about 1938.

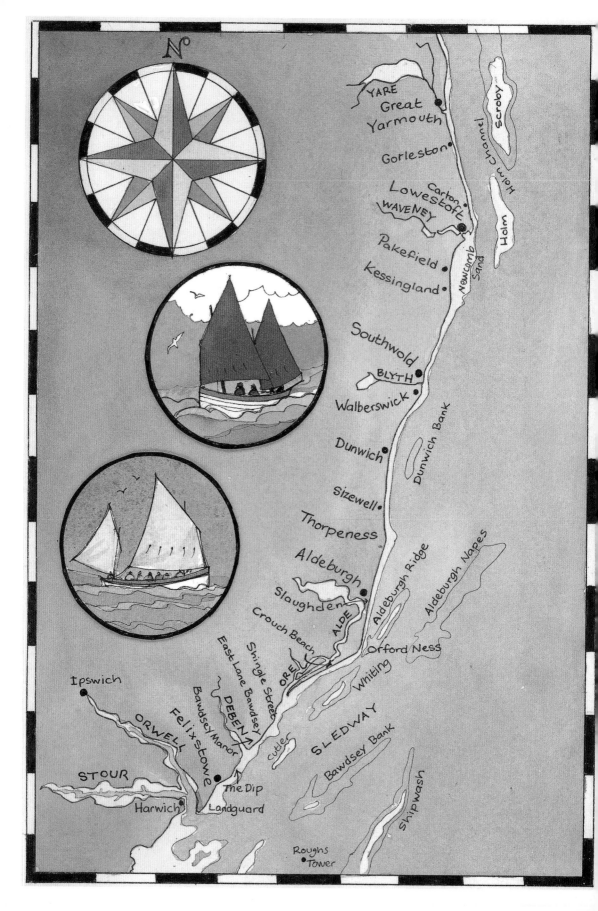

## Felixstowe

### The Undercliff

Felixstowe grew up as a Victorian seaside resort in the railway era, on the claim that because it faced south it was warmer than the rest of the Suffolk coast. Victorian photographs show that the beach was steep and by 1900 the bay was lined with wooden groynes. Early in the twentieth century the Promenade was constructed from near Landguard up to Cobbold's Point. The large house on the Point, which also had a small jetty, was the home of John Chevallier Cobbold, brewer and railway promoter.

By 1900 a group of small open boats ran pleasure trips for summer visitors from the most sheltered part of the beach, just East of the Pier. The largest of these gunter rigged boats was the *Moss Rose*.

Felixstowe was a grand resort with smart hotels along the cliff top, culminating with Douglas Tollemache's Felix Hotel built in 1903. In the 1930s Felixstowe was still a smart resort, but after the creation of the Aldeburgh Festival the affluent visitors moved up the coast to picturesque Aldeburgh and Southwold.

When there was less trade to the port of Woodbridge before World War 1, the Newsons, Felixstowe Ferry pilots, started running trips off Undercliff beach. In the 1930s Arthur Newson had two decked pleasure boats, *Deben Viking* and *Orwell Viking*, running trips from their pitch on the Undercliff beach or in bad weather from Felixstowe Ferry. They either went out to sea or up the River Orwell. The Undercliff and The Dip tripper boats used landing stages on wheels that were pushed down into the sea so that passengers could walk aboard. Both Newson's boats went to the Dunkirk Evacuation and I

Felixstowe Promenade in about 1910 with the *Moss Rose* and other tripper boats. These 'sixpenny sickers' only operated in the summer.

Kevin Barrett with the swamped *Anglelaine* just north of Felixstowe Pier in 1999. Brothers Kevin and Steve Barrett started a fresh fish sales stall on Felixstowe Prom. The *Anglelaine* was kept on a mooring, but had dragged ashore on to the beach.

Ruth Ufford's watercolour of 'Dougie' Goodall's hut near the Spa Pavilion, Felixstowe.

was told that the *Deben Viking* was sunk, but the *Orwell Viking* was still running trips in the early 1950s. The great cry of the Felixstowe boatmen working from Undercliff beach was 'Any more for round the Cork Lightship.'

Dougie Goodall was the last man operating a tripper boat from Felixstowe beach. He also kept and open boat at Felixstowe Ferry for fishing. When the weather was fine he went off after crab, lobster, skate and Dover sole and in the winter he went after cod. In 1947 Dougie had taken over a shed on the beach near the Spa Pavilion for selling the fish he had caught. He used to sit on a bench, which he called his 'office,' and chatted to the public.

Dougie's open yellow boat was a familiar sight off Cobbold's Point where he hauled lobster pots on the rocky seabed. By the time he died in 1997 his catches had fallen so much that fishing had become virtually a hobby, but Dougie just loved being out in his boat.

Peter Fryer, who had helped Dougie, continued the fishing and retail operation here, but this had a setback in 2000 when, one Saturday night, vandals set fire to the shed. This was replaced later.

In the late nineteenth century there was erosion around Cobbold's Point and it appears that this was overcome by selling sections of the beach to people living in big houses in the area; which were not necessarily near the sea. The deeds said they owned as far out as a man could ride on a horse, but it didn't say whether this was at high tide or low tide. The owners of the beach had to maintain the groynes and this seems to have worked for a while, but in the end the council decided to take over all the groynes.

The Felixstowe sea front had long had problems with erosion and concrete groynes had been tried to keep down the maintenance costs. Bad gales in 1986 moved much of the shingle off the Felixstowe beach. Councillor Andy Smith fought to get Government money for long-term protection of Felixstowe. In about 2000 he battled through all Government attempts to stop money going on sea defences

and obtained grey stone groynes for Felixstowe front. This totally altered the appearance of the beach and at first looked rather formidable, but quite quickly the beach grew up again. The old beach was mostly shingle, but sand built up as well and in the flood, December 6, 2013 so much sand washed up on the Prom that it took three weeks to clear away.

Cobbold's Point is heavily defended against the sea and a small harbour was created where the Felixstowe Volunteer Patrol Rescue Service used to operate their inflatable rib *Volunteer* during the summer. John Cresswell started this voluntary service in 1997. Their base moved to Levington and they continue to patrol the Felixstowe sea front and the rivers Orwell and Deben, giving assistance to people and boats in difficulty.

## *The Dip*

The road from Felixstowe to Felixstowe Ferry dips down just after the site of Blackenberry Fort, now a green, and rises up to a car park on the East Cliff just before the golf club. Soon after World War II my grandmother Turner bought a beach hut at The Dip so that her grandchildren could play on the beach there. I loved this place. It was then very rural, with just a wooden hut under the fir trees where sweets were sold.

One of the highlights of my visits to The Dip had been a trip out on the open pleasure boat that the Ford family operated from a jetty that they had wheeled down into the sea. On a calm day we went aboard the Cork Lightship and looked around. I remember it had a cannon for warning ships when they were getting too near to the Cork Sands.

Once we failed to make the Cork Lightship, as the wind had picked up. One of the Fords, at the tiller, explained that the rough sea was due to 'wind over tide.' As a ten-year-old boy I had no idea that it meant that the wind being against the tide was pushing up the waves. The boat rolled and a young mother and her baby kept being sick.

The Dip at Old Felixstowe 2013. The remains of Walton Castle are in the middle of the bay just in line with the mast on the Bawdsey shore. In the distance, fourteen miles away, Orfordness lighthouse can just be seen.

The *Three Sisters* sailing over the Deben Bar in fine weather.

The *Deben Ferry* pulling a yacht back into the channel over the Deben Bar, 2014.

The Gap in Bawdsey Manor cliff has a sheltered beach where smugglers are reputed to have landed goods in the eighteenth century. Peter Sproxton keeps a boat on this new beach landing.

Isaac 'Ikie' Ford and his future wife Sarah Lennard with his lobster boat *Pegasus* at the Landmark landing Bawdsey in 1903. The *Pegasus* has the central mast of the smaller boats used between Felixstowe Ferry and Shingle Street.

The Fords had lived in Bawdsey, where they had a fishing boat on the beach, but they moved to Felixstowe to operate the pleasure launch from a mooring at Felixstowe Ferry.

On very low tides we used to watch people swimming out to the 'Old Roman Fort.' The Romans had trouble with Saxon pirates coming across from North Germany and raiding southeast England. To try and solve this problem they built a series of forts around the coast. The site of one of the Roman Forts was on the high ground over looking the entrance to the River Deben. In the medieval period the Roman fort was rebuilt as Walton Castle, but the headland eroded away and by 1760 Walton Castle was just masonry on the foreshore. In 1969 there was an underwater exploration of the site and it was decided that this was the remains of a gatehouse on the landward side.

This area has always been very prone to erosion and in about 1900 the Pretyman Estate protected the coast with faggots that were made from alder branches bound together. These were used to form groynes and also protect the bottom of the cliff. My grandmother's hut was at the bottom of the cliff with a concrete path in front. In 1989 this whole area was remodelled with a steep concrete revetment, complete with concrete ledges for more beach huts. There was also a small concrete area for leisure boats to be kept in and material to make up the beach was brought in by the dredger *Zeeland*.

The Landmark beach Bawdsey, in 2011, after a bad gale. In the 1880s Quilter started building his country house, Bawdsey Manor, and ten years later he had the groyne field built in front of the Manor, to stop erosion. These helped to build the beach up with shingle, but a hundred years later the groynes were is bad repair, shingle moved away and the whole beach and cliff eroded right up to East Lane.

East Lane, Bawdsey in about 1907, with the boatshed and fishermen's hut.

East Land Point, Bawdsey in about 1910 before the cottages went into the sea. The Quilter Estate had the Promenade built after this to break the force of waves.

## Felixstowe Ferry

Felixstowe Ferry was originally a beach settlement just inside of the mouth of the River Deben, where the men made a precarious living fishing, piloting, salvaging and beachcombing.

In the Victorian era Felixstowe Ferry was the most southerly place on the Suffolk coast where men clubbed together to save lives and salvage ships in distress. There were just informal groups on the southern end of the Suffolk coast, but further north the beach companies were well organised. These groups were able to take far higher financial rewards than they could ever have earned in longshore fishing.

In 1824 there were over 2,000 ships and 20,000 men lost in shipwrecks in the North Sea, and that was just during one year. Since the ships in the coal trade from the north of England passed the coast of East Anglia on their way to the ports in southern England, many ships were wrecked here. The beach company's first objective was to save lives, but after that they were interested in salvage for reward.

Beach companies had huts on the beach with a lookout, and they often met in a pub to share salvage money and make decisions. The companies had to have good crews and fast seaworthy boats to go off the beaches in all weather, and of course a good solicitor to fight their cases in court. Salvaging was big business and groups of working fishermen used to employ the top solicitors of their area to fight their cases.

Little was ever written down about the Suffolk beach companies, but in the mid-Victorian period they were very active and highly profitable. The beach company at Felixstowe Ferry didn't have a name or headquarters, but was a group of longshoremen working together. They had the transom sterned galley, *Pride of the Deben*, which was kept in front of the Martello Tower U, and a smack anchored inside the Horse Sand.

As well as salvage work the *Pride of the Deben's* day job was to go out near the Sunk Lightship and put the pilots Tom 'Bassy' Newson and

Clark onto ships that were bound for the Thames. In 1884 the steamer *Bedder* went ashore on the Shipwash Sands. The *Jane* from Orford Haven (Shingle Street) and the *Pride of the Deben* co-operated with a lifeboat and two tugs to get her off and share in the salvage money. Only a few days later the screw steamer *Enrique de Calvet* went ashore on the Shipwash. The boats that went to her assistance were the Aldeburgh North Company's yawl *Wentworth*, Langmaid's *Jane* from Shingle Street and the *Pride of the Deben*. They all co-operated in getting her afloat and shared the salvage money. In 1889 Ablet Passiful's *Pride of the Deben* took a 5cwt (quarter of a ton) anchor out to the Newcastle brig *Ismyr* that was ashore on the Cutler and kedged her off. The brig's owner's offer was £10 but the court awarded £50.

In 1984 I met the Deben Bar Pilot, Billy Newson, and he remembered seeing the *Pride of the Deben* and her capstan near the Martello Tower. At one stage Billy's father had been in charge of this galley and the story handed down was that the last time they went out was to a large ship abandoned on the Shipwash. They had loaded the *Pride of the Deben* up with cutlery, whisky and a piano. On the way back some of the crew started drinking whisky and by the time they got to Felixstowe Ferry they lay drunk in the bottom of boat.

In the nineteenth century the 15ft pilot and lobster boats at the Ferry were kept on the beach in front of the houses inside the bar across the mouth of the River Deben. These open lugsail boats with light masts were unique, because when tacking against the wind the sail was dropped, the mast lifted up and the sail pushed under it on to the new leeward side. The sail was then re-hoisted.

Many of the sailing lobster boats were ruined during World War I because an army officer thought they would be useful to invading Germans troops and had them stored in a fresh water marsh 'delf' ditch, over the river wall, where they rotted away.

After the Great War new lobster boats were

built with standing lugsails which didn't have to be lowered when tacking. Probably the last man working a sailing lobster boat from the Ferry was 'Jockey' Hunt, who lived near the ferry landing in a small, tarred boat with a hut on it. His hard life caused him to look older than he probably was. In 1952 we came across Jockey out near the Cutler Bank where he had just finished hauling his lobster hoops and was about to row two miles back to the Ferry. We gave him a tow and all the way back he sat in his old boat bailing her out.

In 1960 'Pop' Pearce sold the Felixstowe Ferry Boatyard to Henry Fox of Ipswich. Here Trevor Moore developed a type of 18ft clinker lobster boat with high bows for motoring into the waves. In 1968 Trevor and John White built the 18ft *Eileen R*, larch on oak, for Duncan Read who named her after his mother. At the same time they built the 18ft *Moonraker*, now *Maggie*.

In the *Moonraker* Tam Grundy went trawling for plaice in 'the Bay,' north of Shingle Street and 'off the Harbour,' (the Deben mouth). He even went near Sizewell Bank, fifteen miles away from the Ferry. Tam also went longlining for cod around the Rough Towers, and gutted the fish on the way back. If the fishing was bad on these grounds he sometimes commuted north to go trawling with Tootsie who fished from Aldeburgh. After steaming about an hour and a half north on a spring ebb tide, he used to leave his boat anchored near the North Napes while they went trawling. Eventually the prices had collapsed and there was little return for many hours of hard work. Tam bought the tug/work boat *Ben Michael*, and left the uncertainties of longshore fishing.

In 1972 Tony 'Doogle' Cheek had the 18ft *Douglas* built, at the Ferry Boatyard, with mahogany planks on the topsides and larch planking below the waterline. Doogle once failed to return to the Ferry when fishing in bad weather and a search was made for him. However he had run north before the sea and finished up in Southwold. One night in the 'Victoria' pub Doogle sold the *Douglas* for £1000 and departed to Mousehole, Cornwall to continue fishing there.

The next step at the Ferry Boatyard was to use the same moulds for the width, but lengthen the hull to build 19ft lobster boats. The last two wooden boats built, side-by-side in 1989, with larch planks and oak frames, were the workboat for the yard and the *Ellen*. The Ferry Harbour Master, John White, uses the *Ellen*.

The last licensed pilots at the Deben entrance were Billy and 'Settler' Newson and they had a Pilot's Hut on the point near the ferry landing. In the shed they had a stove for making cups of tea and kept the paraffin lamps that were fixed on the 'Meets' (posts) at night. Two lights were lined up to guide vessels though the channel over the bar. In bad weather the pilot used to stand on the beach and signal with flags to steer the vessels in. The Victorian Pilot's Hut was swept away in the 1953 Flood and replaced by two beach huts put together. In 2014 a two-storey lookout building replaced these.

In the early 1950s I used to crew with the Rev Will Groom on his Edwardian gaff schooner *Lora* and we always took a pilot over the Deben Bar. The Rev Groom phoned up the night before so that the pilot would meet the *Lora* in his launch and we followed him through the channel over the bar. Once through the channel the pilot came alongside for a payment. At that time yachtsmen usually took, and paid, the pilot because 'they wanted him to be there when they needed him.' The Deben Bar had such a bad reputation that not many yachts came in.

Most of the early yachts had low powered engines, but in the 1960s reliable engines and echo sounders became available. With the introduction of fibreglass hulls the number of yachts increased and skippers no longer worried about taking the pilot. Although the Deben Bar is buoyed the channel does move all the time and with the strong tides it is very easy to be in the wrong place. Even on a flood tide a yacht can be swept up on to the shingle knolls and when it is 'wind against tide' it is a murderous place.

Local fishermen are used to towing yachts off the Deben Bar for a payment. In the 1980s Charlie Brinkley had a hut on the Point where he sat and watched the bar channel. Many yachtsmen were very glad of his timely arrival in his ferryboat *Odd Times* to pull them off for a payment. In 2002 the channel changed to its most southerly position, almost down to the golf clubhouse, and was very narrow. Pilot Duncan Read was on call for every daylight flood tide through the peak summer months and had plenty of work pulling yachts off the Knolls. Local workboats still race down to be the first to put a rope aboard a stranded yacht. The spirit of the old beach companies lives on at Felixstowe Ferry.

## Bawdsey

### *The Manor Cliff*
In the book 'Margaret Catchpole' a smuggler's cave in Bawdsey Cliff is mentioned. Local legend said this cave was reached by going down a well at Lower Barn(Dairy Farm). When the 'Margaret Catchpole' first appeared in 1845 the Rev Richard Cobbold stated that it was all true, but many local people complained that it was all fiction. There really was an Ipswich servant girl called Margaret Catchpole who had dressed up as a man, (which the Victorian public found fascinating,) stole a horse, rode to London and tried to sell it. For her crime she was transported to Australia where she became a midwife in Richmond. The Rev Richard Cobbold had grown up in Ipswich and Margaret had worked for his family and he appears to have woven a story around her life using all the tales he had heard of smugglers

### *The Land Mark*
When the East Lane landing had been washed away the Bawdsey fishermen moved south towards the cliff and had their winches and sheds at the Land Mark (sometimes called the Sea Mark.) There was a Sea Mark on the cliffs

Hundred-year-old faggots on Bawdsey beach, probably put there by the Quilter's Beach Gang.

The sea breaking over the Quilter 'Prom' on February 5, 2014 at East Lane, Bawdsey. In 2009 Norwegian rocks had to be brought in to try to halt erosion.

Jonathan and Harry Simper catching herring for supper on *Three Sisters* in 2003.

Harry Simper on *Our Boys* 2015. He was returning from longlining for cod outside the Cutler Bank.

The Cup won by Charlie Burwood reads 'Shinglestreet Regatta, Aug 26 1892, presented by Mrs T.Sibeth.'

Charlie Lucock and Charlie Burwood shaking herring out of a drift net, at Shingle Street, in about 1925. There were then five boats working off the beach and children used to race home from school to help walk round the capstans to pull boats up the beach.

Will Lucock going out to a yacht to pilot her out of Orford Haven in 1930. This Shingle Street boat obviously had a centre mast as one of the strops, to connect the sail, is hanging over the bow.

The *Pet* off Bawdsey in 2011.

Olly Hind, Harry Simper and Tim Bradford in the *Pet*, with one reef down, passing a lobster pot buoy off Shingle Street.

The Coastguard Cottages at Shingle Street in 1962. The old river mouth that had formed into 'ponds' had gone into the sea in just over a decade. The boat *IH100* in the distance belonged to Don Potter.

at Bawdsey on a 1552 chart to give ships a bearing for the Sledway between the Whiting Bank and the Bawdsey Bank. Later a brick Land Mark was built, but this was pulled down in 1934 because the cliff was eroding away. The site of the Land Mark and the pond beside it are now out under the sea.

The Bawdsey men had small open lobster boats with a lugsail almost amidships, but sometimes they spent all day rowing. They got crabs and whelks with their hoop nets and the boys from the village used to gather firewood for the coppers they cooked them in. The boys were rewarded with crabs for their efforts. Most of the whelks were sold around the villages but some were taken in bags, on bicycle handlebars, across the ferry to Felixstowe Station. Here they were put on the train to Billingsgate, where they were sold as East Lane Whelks.

The last Bawdsey fishermen appear to have bought their boats with the gratuities for fighting in World War I. In the 1930s these were Len Francis, 'Talo' Friend who was born and lived in the Martello Tower towards Shingle Street and also a 'shima'ca' (shoemaker), then there was Toby Hunt who lived in a hut beside the East Lane. He used to sit there watching us go to school in the early 1940s, and then one day we were told that he had died in the night. I felt as if my hair stood on end every time I ran past his hut. I think the last man working a boat was 'Iky' Ford who had an open boat called *Pegasus* until 1939. The hand winch used to pull the boats up the beach was still there in the 1980s.

## East Lane

Because sailing ships sheltered in Hollesley Bay, Bawdsey was one of the first places to have a lifeboat. In 1801 a 30ft lifeboat was placed at East Lane and in 1816 she was used to rescue the crew of the Yarmouth schooner *Ruby* that sank on the 'Bawdsey Flats.' This vessel may have been the wooden sailing ship hulk that began to show up in front of Bawdsey Manor on a very low spring tide in the early 1980s. The Bawdsey lifeboat was moved from East Lane to the Deben entrance, probably where the dinghy park of the Bawdsey Haven Yacht Club is sited.

This lifeboat was withdrawn in 1853 because of the difficulties in getting a crew.

The legend in Bawdsey was that cattle were once driven down to graze on the marshes past East Lane, now out under the sea. Early nineteenth century maps refer to this area as being the Boathouse Point, but again all this went into the sea. By 1880 Bawdsey fishermen had two capstans on the beach about quarter of a mile to the north. The boats, sheds and capstans appear to have been moved to the end of East Lane when the Coastguard Cottages were built there. Although the coast must have been fairly stable for the cottages to be built there they had gone within about twenty-five years.

The shopkeeper in Bawdsey Street used to put a light in a back window when he knew that the men were out fishing at night. The light was also used by the 'Southwoldies' who came down fishing in their open boats, as far as Woodbridge Haven (Deben entrance.)

The Felixstowe Ferry fisherman Charlie Brinkley, who grew up at Bawdsey Quay in the 1920s, had heard the old men talking about the East Lane landing. The point was then far enough out for the boats to launch on the Hollesley Bay side. Charlie also said they had their own beach company and galley. Sadly I have never found any more information on the. East Lane Beach Company; it was probably very informal and they used to settle up in the 'Star' in Bawdsey afterwards. A 1907 photograph shows a boat larger than the fishing boats outside a boathouse under a cover and this might have been a galley used for collecting wreckage and salvage work.

Sir Cuthbert Quilter started to develop East Lane as a holiday resort called Bawdsey-on-Sea and tried unsuccessfully to bring a railway line here from Melton. This all ended in 1912 when the land had been eaten away and the row of Coastguard Cottages, two boathouses and the beach huts had gone into the sea.

The Quilter Estate promised that every man in their villages would have work, and one of their schemes was to form a Beach Gang to maintain the groynes. In the winter the fishermen were glad of a job in the Beach Gang, barrowing shingle on the beach that had moved. The groynes were successful at holding the beach in place, but as the remains of the point were still threatened the Quilter Estate brought in a Dutch engineer and built a massive sea defence known as 'The Prom.' The Quilter Estate halted the erosion and held the sea back for half a century, but the cost nearly ruined the Estate.

Just after World War II the shingle started to move again and in about 1947 the school children used to hear a pile driver hammering in the groynes, just south of the Prom. This held the sea back but when the groynes needed repair the authorities took the extraordinary decision to pull them out rather than repair them. The result was that the shingle moved off the south beach and exposed the whole of Bawdsey cliff to erosion.

In 2004 Bawdsey was in serious trouble again but the authorities abandoned East Lane and stepped back to allow a large part of the coast to be flooded. Eventually this would have led to the hamlet of Shingle Street going into the sea.

Local landowners, the Mann family and A.W.Mortier Farms, took advice from Gerry Matthews, who had worked in the oil industry, to create the East Lane Trust. The landowners gave land to sell for housing developments and this raised money for the sea defences

The East Lane Trust was a pioneering idea not seen in the United Kingdom before. This encouraged the Government to repeat the idea in other places so that local people have become expected to contribute to the cost of sea defences. This is unique because the Government pays for all other forms of national defence.

The idea of paying for sea defence by undertaking housing development was acceptable in Bawdsey and Alderton, where people could see the sea and understand its threat, but in Hollesley, just inland, people did not relate to the danger of the sea. There was very bitter opposition to the building of new housing on green field sites to pay for coastal defences. Later when the idea was tried in Norfolk to re-house people on a green field site inland this was strongly opposed. Erosion does not just affect the coastal area; the impact is on the wider community.

## Bawdsey Beach

Bawdsey Beach runs from East Lane to Shingle Street which is part of the parish of Bawdsey, One of the Bawdsey beach fishermen used to say that there had been a track, now under the sea, with gorse growing on it on either side, linking Shingle Street to the rest of Bawdsey. Apart from walkers and anglers not many people visit this lonely stretch of steep shingle beach. There is a track across the marshes and up Beach Lane to The Knoll in the centre of Alderton. The legend in Alderton is that the eighteenth century smugglers used to come up Beach Lane during the night. This is probably true because there is a smuggler's tunnel, now blocked at either end, linking the church with Alderton Hall, the adjoining farmhouse. It is recorded that in 1784 the 1st Regiment of the Dragoon Guards seized over 250 gallons of brandy and Geneva gin in Alderton and managed to get it back to Melton safely. However about forty Bawdsey and Alderton smugglers got away. It seems that the authorities eventually stopped the smuggling gang by building a three-storey house in Alderton Street where they could watch the lane and the beach. When the smuggling was stamped out the house was pulled down. The 'Swan' in Alderton has some old smuggling artefacts.

During a storm tide in 1906 the sea broke through Bawdsey Beach and flooded the marsh level between Bawdsey and Hollesley. This flood was a serious blow to local farmers and it also temporarily destroyed a great deal of fresh water bird habitat. An old sailing barge was towed from Ipswich and sunk across the gap and shingle soon built up around it.

In October 1916 the 80ft sailing barge *Emma Mizzen* anchored off Orford Haven with a cargo of flints, waiting for the flood tide to go into the River Ore. The wind turned into a strong North Easterly the *Emma Mizzen's* anchor chain broke and she was driven ashore near East Lane. The bargemen tried to get ashore in their boat, but it overturned in the breakers. The Shingle Street men had been watching and ran along the beach in time to pull the bargemen out of the water.

In the early 1980s a man living in Bawdsey used to keep a small angling boat on the shingle beach. It became impossible to land a boat here after the arrival of stone from Norway to stop erosion.

# Shingle Street

The Medieval fishermen kept boats in Hollesley Haven, now called Barthorp's Creek, which went into Hollesley Bay. There appear to have been fishermen's houses on the coast but these were washed away. Later on no one wanted to live on the coast because of the raids by the Dunkirkers, French pirates who were eventually suppressed by the Royal Navy.

The first house on the ridge of shingle that became Shingle Street, appears to have been the Pilot's House built in about 1800. Technically Shingle Street is a part of Bawdsey Parish because it was once linked to that village by a track along the beach with gorses growing on either side. When a bridge was built across Barthorp's Creek another track was made across the Oxley Marshes linking the beach to Hollesley and Woodbridge.

The line of single storey cottages dotted along the shingle ridge beside the beach often contained wood from ships wrecked on Orfordness and timber that had been lost overboard from ships coming from Scandinavia. The occupants were able to earn a modest living by servicing passing ships, piloting and fishing. Much of the fishing was simply done to feed their families.

A young dead whale ashore at Shingle Street, 2012. In medieval times stranded whales were eaten.

The morning after the December 6 2013 surge tide with the tide line behind the 1881 Coastguard Cottages at Shingle Street. The abnormal tide had broken through the beach and the harbour wall so that for three tides the road to Shingle Street was flooded.

In 1849 the pilot Francis Langmaid became landlord of the 'Lifeboat Inn'. This then overlooked the entrance of the River Ore and had a jetty where mariners could land. Langmaid had the old smack *Jemina* and used to organise a salvage group. The salvaged goods from the ship *Robinson* earned him enough money to buy the transom sterned, open galley *Jane*, and several salvages were made with her.

The last time the *Jane* was taken out was to try to help a brig ashore on the Shipwash Sands. The Scottish Master of the brig refused to let them get aboard as he hoped that the brig would float off with the next tide. The Shingle Street men said 'We left in a hurry, could we have some water to drink.' As the Master thought that this was a trick to get aboard and claim salvage he refused to have them aboard. He looked down and saw water in the bottom of the leaking *Jane* and shouted; 'You've got plenty in there, drink that.' After this the *Jane* was kept on the lagoon in front of the houses and in the 1920s the children used to play in her.

Another form of salvage that the Shingle Streeters practiced was to take coal out of the numerous wrecks around Orfordness. They had a huge underwater 'spoon' that they worked between two boats, to fish the coal out of the wrecks. The men also used to load barges with shingle for the construction of docks in the north of England. The barges were put ashore against the steep shingle beach and the men barrowed shingle down a plank with wheelbarrows. There was a great art in walking in step with the bouncing plank. If a man got it wrong, he and the barrow were thrown down on to the beach.

There had been plans to bring a railway line to Shingle Street so that it could be developed as a holiday resort. In 1883, and again a few years later, huge tides broke through the shingle and the 'Harbour' river wall. This wall at the entrance to the River Ore had been constructed in about 1790 by local landowners. It stretches from the Coastguard Cottages to 'The Cri'k'

(Barthorp's Creek,) and was built to protect the grazing marshes. Once through the Harbour Wall the tide flooded the Oxley Marshes and in effect turned Shingle Street into an island. Wealthy families were already coming to Shingle Street for summer holidays and had promoted the idea of a railway link to create a holiday resort, but the 1880s floods ended the plan of a railway line to the coast.

The Norton brothers owned the ancient schooner *Rudolf*, which was wrecked before their eyes. In 1895 she had arrived off Shingle Street, with coal from Hartlepool, bound for Boyton Dock. Alfred 'Taffy' Norton was the skipper and the pilot was Will Lucock. As there was no wind they followed the normal practice of drifting in on the tide with the anchor dragging along the bottom, but the strong tide swept her on the knolls. Here she sat on her anchor and sank. As she was not insured she was left there and became buried by the shingle. In 1952 I went swimming in the sea at Shingle Street at low tide and found the exposed bows of the *Rudolf* in the shingle at the bottom of the beach The hulk of the *Rudolf* was almost in front of the site of the 'Lifeboat Inn.'

In 1897 a huge tide broke through the shingle to form a new river entrance north of the houses and the old mouth became a hugh 'pond'.

The force of the tide hitting the shallow bars across the mouths to the rivers Deben, Ore and the Blyth can be over powering. Steep breaking waves caused a disaster at Shingle Street in 1914 when five Coastguards were drowned within sight of their homes. The Coastguards had been to Aldeburgh in their open cutter to collect stores and wages. Before returning they had visited the 'Three Mariners Inn' at Slaughden and the 'Jolly Sailor' at Orford. They landed on the North Weir at the Victorine Hut and rang up the Shingle Street Coastguard Station. They were warned that there was a dangerous sea running on the Ore Bar and it shouldn't be crossed.

However the coxswain of the cutter, Chief Officer Mauger, decided to sail out of the river, over the bar, and land on the beach in front of the Coastguard Cottages. Perhaps this was because it would have been easier to land on the sea beach, rather than carry all the stores over the shingle from the river.

As the cutter approached the breaking water on the Bar the coxswain lost control in the fierce tide. They quickly dropped the sail and mast, but before they could get the oars out and regain control the cutter capsized in the breakers. Five men were lost in a few minutes, but the boatman McCauley managed to get his overcoat off just before the cutter turned over and was able to swim and drag boatman Goble ashore on to a knoll. Two boatmen from the Coastguard Station then rescued them.

The Shingle Streeters lived hard but independent lives, on the edge of the world between sea and marshes. The women spent a lot of time 'shoring,' beachcombing for any thing useful washed up. Poaching was both a necessity and a hobby. The men went out for food for their families and often used rifles, because they were silent. They shot geese, pheasants or anything else edible. The pilot Will Lucock was respected because he could outrun any of the local gamekeepers.

Two wealthy families used to spend the summer at the settlement on the shingle beach and this brought employment, particularly to women taking in washing. The summer visitors put up the funds for the Shingle Street Colonial Regatta. In one Regatta Charlie Burwood won a cup. When he died in 1929 his *Snowdrop* was the last Shingle Street boat on the beach without an engine. In 1923 Robertsons of Woodbridge built the first Shingle Street boat with an engine. This was the *Lassie*, built for Charlie Lucock and named after his dog. Charlie Lucock died of cancer as a young man and the *Lassie* was sold to the Alderton butcher Jack Garrard. The *Lassie* was the first boat that I remember going afloat in. This was just after World War II, and as she leaked it became my job to keep her pumped out at Ramsholt.

The last sailing boat working at Shingle Street was the *Gem*. Eric Andrews, who was the last pilot at the river mouth, had her built in about 1938 by Everson of Woodbridge. The *Gem* had a central mast, unique to Hollesley Bay and the Deben mouth, so that when tacking against the wind the lug could be dipped by lowering it, lifting the mast up, pushing the sail under and rehoisting it on the leeward side. She also had a hook inside the bow on either side for the lugsail to be fastened to. When Eric couldn't get out to a craft coming in over the bar, he used to guide them in by signalling them in with flags from the beach.

In 1940 Shingle Street beach was fenced off with barbed wire as far as the Deben entrance. The beach was also mined as an invasion of German troops had been expected at any moment. While this was being carried out, one soldier from the Liverpool Scottish Regiment was killed when a mine blew up.

The whole coast became a military zone and people in the twenty-three houses at Shingle Street were given a day to pack up and leave. An army lorry was sent to collect all the people, mostly women and children, who had to find accommodation in the Hollesley area. Four Shingle Street Coastguards had to return daily to watch the coast.

The Shingle Streeters were told that their houses would be locked up and the army promised, but not in writing that everything would be there when they returned after the War. However the British soldiers broke into the houses and looted the homes, mainly for firewood. Damage was also done when the army was experimenting with a fire that got out of control and killed one soldier. This was an embarrassment to the army and appears to be the reason why some World War II details about Shingle Street were not revealed.

Once, when I was a small boy, I was cycling behind my mother on the high ground in Hollesley. It was a clear day and I saw a lone plane dive down on Shingle Street and release a 'bomb.' My mother told me that was not interesting and I must hurry up. Presumably the plane was on a practice bombing flight. I gather that another time some Shingle Street people came out of Hollesley Church one morning and saw their homes being bombed by our planes.

During World War II the Suffolk beaches were used as shingle quarries for the urgently needed construction work. At Shingle Street two concrete roads were hastily made, one down to the Beacon bungalow and the other across the 'pond', the old mouth of the River Ore, on a ridge of shingle in front of the houses. Thousands of tons of shingle were carted away from Shingle Street for Debach Aerodrome. Unfortunately this was done in such haste that driftwood and rubbish were left in the shingle and some runways had to be rebuilt. Whether this triggered off erosion or not is debatable, but the sea eroded the lagoon away so that the houses were on the sea beach.

After the war the Government claimed that Shingle Street was so badly 'war damaged' that the settlement should be abandoned. This plan was thwarted by a vigorous campaign by Kate Burwood who demanded to go back home and for the Government to rebuild their houses. The Government reluctantly rebuilt the houses, but charged the Shingle Streeters 'Betterment' for the new brick houses.

Fishing from the beach at Shingle Street had always been just one of the ways that men had earned a living. It was often a way of feeding their families, but after World War II fishing became a leisure activity. Eric Andrews already had the *Gem* and for his next boat simply reversed his family's initials to *Meg*. Don Potter, landlord of the 'Shepherd and Dog' in Hollesley, owned the *IH100*, a 'proper Aldeburgh Boat,' and used her for trawling. Ron Harris had an angling boat and Paul Maskell had a boat with an outboard. He used to go lobstering about half a mile off the beach and out near the Cutler Bank. The lobster grounds were found by lining up Bawdsey Church with the end Martello Tower, and this line was crossed with Hollesley church.

Shingle Street fishermen's trawling grounds had been 'The Bay', from the Ore Bar towards Orfordness lighthouse, but eventually larger beam trawlers came in and more or less mopped up everything from these grounds.

Norman Smealing kept an ex-Commando's dory, which later became Vic Clouting's *Veegee*, near the Coastguard Cottages. Several of these wartime dories turned up on the coast just after World War II and were used by fishermen until they could afford boats with more space. These dories were built to be stacked up on a destroyer's deck and were used to sneak ashore. They had huge silencers in the bilges and starter keys in a box so as not to give off an electrical signal.

The shingle kept moving and the beach moved right back so that on a high tide debris was swept right up to the path (the shingle street) in front of the cottage garden fences. On a high tide, the sea also seeped under the houses and ran out on to the road behind. Shingle Street looked doomed; it seemed to be just a matter of time before the sea burst through onto the Oxley grazing marshes.

In 1965 22,000 tons of shingle were carted from Landguard Point by lorry and put in front of the Coastguard Cottages. This technique does not always work, but here it was a very wise investment by the authorities as the beach started to build up and extend out in front of houses again.

In about 1986 Philip and James Green had a go at reviving commercial fishing at Shingle Street in the ex-Thorpeness boat *Our Soles*. They went after cod, trammel netted outside the Cutler and further offshore went tangle netting for dogfish.

Once shingle had started to pile up in front of the houses it continued further out, making it very difficult to work a boat from here. However the new residents that had moved into Shingle Street had no interest in longshore fishing. When an estate agent tried to get them to bid for individual plots of land behind the houses Bruce Page and

Playing dominoes in the 'Jolly Sailor,' Orford, in about 1961. Landlord Sid Harper is behind the bar and left to right Joe Thacker, Tom Ellis, Joe Simpson, Tom Brinkley and George Brinkley.

David Williams rallied everyone together to form the Shingle Street Settlement Company. Each house has shares in the ownership of the land surrounding the houses. These shares cannot be sold separately as they pass on with the house ownership. This gives the hamlet a great sense of cooperation.

The Environment Agency gave two days warning of very high tides for December 6 2013 and Shingle Street residents planned to go to the Martello Tower. Fortunately their houses remained safe and dry on the shingle ridge. In the morning they saw that the Oxley Marshes were flooded behind them and that the sea had broken through the beach, near the Beacon bungalow and then broken through the Harbour Wall. For three tides Shingle Street was cut off and by then the Environment Agency had filled the gap in the beach and the river wall.

# Orford

## Orford Beach

When Orford Castle was built in 1173 it overlooked the entrance of the River Ore. It is probable that the devout medieval people put up a Crouch (cross) at the entrance, just below Stonyditch. In about 1400 there was just open coast, but the movement of shingle formed Orfordness. The movement of the shingle forced the River Ore entrance to move south and gradually formed Orfordness. By the Elizabethan period the entrance was as far down as the Butley River and the changes forced the tide to gouge out another channel, the Gull (Suffolk for a small valley) to form Havergate Island. The mouth continued moving south slowly until the North 'Ear' Point (North Weir Point) reached Shingle Street. This meant that Orford Beach ran from the North 'Ear' Point right up to Orfordness.

The Orfordness Low Light was washed away in a storm in 1887. The north side of the Ness, right up to Slaughden, started to erode away the Low Light was moved in land several times.

The Orfordness High Lighthouse was built in 1792. In about 1839 Orford yawls were based here to attend passing shipping. The High and Low Lights were leading lights to guide ships round the headland clear of the banks.

The narrow Nydam ship of about the year 400 was clearly a rowing boat. In Scandinavia the nineteenth century Church Boats, used to go to church by the community, were still almost the same as this boat.

Pete Benstead standing beside the Orfordness lighthouse in 2014. Andrew Hawes designed the 'shingle sausages' put on the beach to stop the sea encroaching. The Light had been turned off in June the year before.

A Customs Landrover stuck in front of Orfordness Lighthouse in 1992. The lighthouse caretaker, Charlie Underwood is on the right.

Orford Beach is the loneliest coastline in Suffolk and it would be surprising if nineteenth century smuggling gangs had not used it. Gwen Dyke knew an elderly lady, daughter of the landlord of the Butley 'Oyster,' whose most treasured procession was small wooden barrel. A smuggler had given the barrel to her, great-great-grandmother in return for keeping quiet. In the eighteenth century John Cook ran the Butley smuggling gang from the 'Oyster' and it is recorded that some of their 'crops' were taken up the Butley River. Certainly when the Customs Service was started the *Victorine* was moored in the River Ore, below Havergate Island, so that the officers could watch this beach. There was also a Coast Guard station on Orford Quay that was used to watch out for smugglers and ships in distress.

In 1823 the Suffolk Association for saving the lives of Shipwreck Sailors had placed the new 23ft self-righting lifeboat *Grafton* on Orford Beach. Later the *Grafton* was moved to Woodbridge Haven, at the mouth of the River Deben.

The 1835 Ordnance Survey map marks the Crouch Life Boat House on the beach beside Hollesley Bay. This was not a practical place to keep a lifeboat, as the crew had to row down the river and walk across the shingle to reach the lifeboat. However, when they launched the lifeboat it would have been near the ships in trouble rounding Orfordness.

Before World War I the only boat builder in the Orford area was Bill Bugg, who worked in a shed behind the Sudbourne 'Chequers'. He was really a wheelwright, but built open fishing boats as a sideline. Bugg built 15ft beach boats, such as *Dot* and *King Edward* and when Charlie 'Hook' Brinkley lived on Havergate Island he had Bugg build him the 13ft *Lizzie*, including oars, sails, anchor, copper nails and bronze fittings for £13.

When beach boats showed signs of age they were often sold for use in the rivers and the moorings at Orford usually have a few. Old wooden hulls fascinated Chris Martin and in his boatyard, just over the river wall at Orford, he rebuilt several. Chris rebuilt the *Julie Ann*, originally built in 1971 by Frank Knights for Rod Markham. Sadly Chris died when he was rebuilding *Our Boys*, and no one else has taken up the challenge of trying to save Suffolk boats.

## Orfordness

The origins of the clinker-built (overlapping planks) wooden boats used to fish off the Suffolk coast go back to the earliest days of northern European culture. Building a clinker hull appears to have started on the shores of the southern Baltic. The first complete clinker built boat was found in 1863, in a bog in Nydam Moss, Schleswig. Nydam was then in Denmark, but after the Prusso-Danish War it became part of Northern Germany. The 73ft Nydam boat that dates from about 400 AD has fine lines. It probably represents the type of craft that was used by the early Anglo-Saxons to cross the North Sea and settle in England.

The Nydam boat was a fast rowing boat, but in 1939 the out line of a much larger Anglo-Saxon longship was found at Sutton Hoo, above the River Deben. All the evidence suggests that this was the burial ship of Raedwald, King of East Anglia, who died in about 625. The Anglo-Saxons had been regularly crossing the North Sea for at least two hundred years before the Sutton Hoo ship was built. The hull of this longship was much fuller amidships than the Nydam ship, presumably to carry a sail to speed up the passage. In 1939 it was believed that because the Sutton Hoo ship did not have a keel she would have just been used for rowing. If there had been a mast case in the hull it would have confirmed that a sail had been used, but the king had been laid to rest in a chamber just where the mast case would have been and all the hull fittings had been removed.

Even in a straight line it is about three hundreds miles from Schleswig Holstein to Suffolk. It would have been impractical for the early Anglo-Saxons to have made regular voyages across the

The Sutton Hoo Anglo-Saxon ship being excavated in 1939. This long ship dates from about 600 and was much more beamier than the Nydam ship, presumably to carry the weight of a mast and sail.

Edwin Gifford and his crew in the 44ft *Sae Wylfing*, a half size replica of the Sutton Hoo ship.

North Sea without using some sail.

The Sutton Hoo ship would have been a rowing and sailing craft and her long extended bow would have lifted the hull at sea and made it easier for the crew to get ashore when running up on a beach. In Gotland, the Danish archaeologist Flemming Riech found a rock carving of longships, of the Sutton Hoo era, with tall square sails.

The Suffolk beach boats descended from these early clinker ships and thirteen hundred years later they were still operated as rowing and sailing boats. They didn't have an extended keel because that would have made it impossible to have run up on a beach. When sailing to windward (against the wind) the men also rowed with an oar over the leeward side to keep the head up into the wind. When tacking they often rowed the head round with an oar. Some Southwold boats had leeboards, particularly for racing.

In 1822 William Daniell produced an aquatint of the two lighthouses on Orfordness. In the foreground there are two black open boats with sloping bow and stern and there appears to be a launching trolley in the background. As there is no fishing gear in sight it is likely that Daniell was portraying two early Orford yawls, which could be launched either side of the Ness. It would appear that the Orford beach company operated from the Ness.

The watercolour by J.M.W. Turner, dated 1830, shows a brig in distress off Orfordness. A crowd of anxious onlookers, relatives and neighbours on the beach, near the lighthouse are watching three yawls pulling towards a brig in distress. Another print of 1838 is of a boat trying to save the *Orion* off Orfordness Low Lighthouse.

The two lighthouses on Orfordness were built after a bad storm in 1661 when thirty-two ships were wrecked on the Ness. The High and Low lighthouses were lined up so that ships could be steered on a safe course down the coast and avoid the shallow banks off Aldeburgh. The Orfordness Low Lighthouse was washed away in a storm in 1887, but the foundations were still visible on the foreshore in the 1950s,

In the 1990s storms began to seriously eat away the Ness point and wash shingle away. A northeast gale in 2012 took away six metres in one night and the following year Trinity House turned off the Orfordness Light and handed the ownership over to Nicholas Gold, a London Barrister with a house in Orford. Nicholas set out to try and preserve this coastal image, but met with opposition from the coastal defeatists, who incredibly seemed happy for the lighthouse to go into the sea.

The back of the 'Three Mariners' at Slaughden in about 1910.

A high tide in 1938 washing past the Hazard House. The sea broke through the Slaughden spit in the 1953 floods, but the line has been successfully held since.

## Slaughden

In 1900 Slaughden had a busy seafaring community on a narrow strip of land just south of Aldeburgh town. It seems that fishermen either worked in the River Alde or at sea. In bad weather the Aldeburgh fishermen used to drag their boats over the shingle and go fishing in the River Alde.

The 'Three Mariners' pub sign at Slaughden was written on whalebone. This had probably been brought home on one of the Aldeburgh smacks in the Icelandic cod fishery. There were also two slaughterhouses, warehouses, a shop, sail makers, boatyard and cottages here. However most of the twenty houses went into the sea within two decades.

Rows of posts were put on the beach to try and save the 'Three Mariners' but even then, on a high spring tide the sea used to wash in the back door and out through the front door. The problem was that when the sea started to encroach Britain was fighting World War I and no one had time, money or energy to fight the sea. In 1923 the 'Three Mariners' was pulled down.

The Hazard was the last occupied at Slaughden and was the home of the marshman who looked after the Lantern Marshes to the south of Slaughden. Every day the marshman went on horseback, two and a half miles, around Lantern Marshes checking the cattle and sheep. The sea broke into The Hazard three times and finally, in 1924, the Ashford family were forced to leave. Three-year-old Ronald was carried out of the house on George Ward's shoulders. Ward had to wade, waist deep, back to Aldeburgh, and this time the family didn't return. Slaughden became a strip of shingle with fishermen's huts. In the 1930s an Aldeburgh fishermen used to row over the site of the cottage where he had been born and see the fresh water bubbling up from the old cottage well.

E. Mill's watercolour of Aldeburgh Moot Hall in 1865. There is a trading sloop, probably belonging to Rope's of Iken, discharging coal into carts on the beach.

The remains of The Hazard were pulled down in 1940 and in the 1953 Flood the sea finally smashed its way over into the River Alde. The fishermen's sheds were all swept away and Stanley Ashford's engineering boatshed vanished with his tools and livelihood. Some of the boats that he had repaired on the beach were swept through the gap into the river. Since then a great effort has gone into keeping the Slaughden strip of land in existence. If the sea got through here permanently it would take out Orfordness, flood the Sudbourne Marshes and begin eating away at the high ground inland. The sea never stops unless man's ingenuity intervenes.

At a meeting of the Suffolk Coastal Forum in the Suffolk Coastal District Council chamber on September 11, 2013, Mick Allen of the Crown Estates suggested to members that the best way to stop erosion was to have a long sloping beach that would take the power out of the waves before they hit the land.

In The Netherlands they have the same problem, but with careful management they have prevented coastal erosion. The latest method there is Sand Engines. In essence these are sacrificial headlands built so that the soil is eroded off the headland and gradually swept along the coast to keep the beaches healthy. The Dutch found that these artificial sand headlands became an attraction for summer visitors.

When Mick Allen announced the Crown Estates plan, Councillor Guy Macgregor, was overjoyed that someone had come up with a long-term solution to Suffolk's ancient problem, but an environmentalist decried it saying that the stones could be the wrong size.

## Aldeburgh

The Suffolk coast is shaped by erosion; every major storm alters the coast somewhere. It is assumed when the Anglo-Saxons settled here there was an old Roman town on the entrance

In the Victorian era the pilots at Aldeburgh built the South Lookout to spot ships at sea.

The 55ft yawl-rigged Aldeburgh pilot cutter *Pilot AI* was built by Hunt at Aldeburgh in 1842. Pilots were put aboard passing ships from the Aldeburgh cutters that stayed at sea.

The transom from the *Joan* of Aldbro that had been one of A.E.Collis' sailing tripper boats. When an engine was fitted, with a central prop, a new sternpost had been added.

to the River Alde at Slaughden and they called it Old Burgh (Aldeburgh). If this is the case the remains of this Roman town lie on the seabed in front of the present town.

It is certain that the sea in front of Aldeburgh was very good for inshore fishing and the easiest way to get to these fish was to launch a boat off the beach. The Elizabethan map of 1588 shows fourteen double-ended sizable boats hauled up and some hand capstans on Aldeburgh beach. These early Aldeburgh beach boats looked, from the simple drawings, to be clinker built double-ended boats similar to the Anglo-Saxon boats.

For centuries sprat and herring were the mainstay of Aldeburgh's fishing economy. In Elizabeth I's reign three hundred men are said to have taken part in the annual 'spratte fare' and even in the Victorian era two hundred men

Charlie Burwood (1840-1916) had two boats and a Chandlery Shop. He had two bowler hats and wore the best one on Sundays. The ballast bags lying on the beach were filled up with shingle to make the boat deeper in the water for sailing. As the boat was filled with fish the shingle was emptied over the side.

The beach at Aldeburgh in about 1906. Beach boats all had bungs to drain the water out when on ashore. In the summer, if not in use, a couple of bucket of salt water was thrown in every day to stop the hull from drying out.

Aldeburgh beach, in about 1937. The beachmen derived an income during the summer by letting out bathing machines, beach huts and the swimming rafts.

Brian Cotton and Tom Parnell getting a beam trawl ready on Aldeburgh beach in 1946. Tom Parnell had started off as a boy working on the Aldeburgh cod smacks.

Jim Cable's *Amy & Jim* landing at Aldeburgh in 1967. While trawling near Orfordness for sea trout, lighting had split her mast and it was not replaced.

Colin Smith's *Dorothy May* landing at Aldeburgh in 1981. The Aldeburgh boats had a wire 'strop' spliced into the keel and this had been hooked on to the end of a wire to pull her up the beach.

Colin 'Tooties' Smith's *Rachael Linda* and *Dorothy May* on Aldeburgh beach in 1990.

manned the boats off Aldeburgh beach in the autumn drift net fishing for sprat and herring.

Aldeburgh was a small, successful medieval town with its 1515 Moot Hall (Town Hall) sitting beside the market place in the middle of the town. Again the sea has eaten its way inland and destroyed two streets so that the Moot Hall is now on the sea front. The Aldeburgh poet George Crabbe witnessed a great storm in 1779 when the seas swept away land and destroyed eleven houses, including the cottage where he had been born.

The loss of Dunwich, half of Aldeburgh and other villages along the coast had a profound effect on the social history of the Suffolk coast. People left because they saw no future in the area. The men who stayed often went to sea for much of the year, but if they could, they returned home to take part in the autumn herring fishery. When drift netting, the boats needed three men, but in the summer, when trawling, a boat could be worked by one or two men.

The open transom sterned two masted luggers probably appeared on the Suffolk coast in the late eighteenth century. When Will Crutten built a 'lugsail boat' at Slaughden in 1803 it was something new to be commented on. In an 1825 watercolour by J. M. W. Turner, of the River Alde at Slaughden, two types of open sailing boats are seen in the river. One of these is double-ended with two masts and looks very Anglo-Saxon, and the other is a smaller transom-sterned beach boat with a small lugsail on the mizzenmast. Turner was recording the older boat type and the newer transom sterned type of 'lug sail' boat that was being adopted and became standard on the Suffolk coast in the nineteenth century. A watercolour of about the same period by Thomas Churchyard (1798-1865) shows what appears to be double-ended, tarred fishing boats on Aldeburgh beach. Churchyard lived in Woodbridge, but was one of a growing number of summer visitors that came to Aldeburgh.

In the mid Victorian period the pilots and fishing were more important to Aldeburgh than summer visitors. The Aldeburgh pilots were

Boats on Aldeburgh beach in 1990. Looking north from here the boats belonged to the Smiths, Jim Cable, Eddie, Bob and Sid Strowger and Billy Burrell's beach was at the top end.

primarily concerned with guiding ships bound into the Thames Estuary ports. There were two companies, based in public houses, which were bitter rivals. The South End Company, the Up Streeters met in the 'Brudenell Tap' and the 'Black Horse' while the North Company, the Down Streeters, met at the 'Cross Keys.'

In 1818 there were fifteen pilots at Aldeburgh with nine yawls to take them out to ships. Originally pilots used to watch from the hill above the town for a ship flying a flag requesting a pilot. In about 1850 the North Aldeburgh Beachmen's Salvage Company built the North Look Out. The South End Company replaced their wooden tower with a three storey brick Lookout on the beach.

Because it was often impossible to launch a boat off the beach in bad weather, the Aldeburgh companies also had decked pilot boats that patrolled at sea. They used to tow 8-oared gigs to make the final dash to reach the ship. An early pilot boat built at Slaughden in 1845 was the *William & Mary* that had an 8ft draft so that she could stay at sea in all weathers.

These decked pilot boats mainly cruised off Orfordness, but sometimes roamed way out into the North Sea looking for a ship bound for London.

William Hunt at Slaughden built the pilot cutter *Maiden* for the Aldeburgh Pilotage & Fishing Co of Slaughden, but she was run down and sunk by a steamer on her maiden voyage. Hunt also built the eight-oared pilot gig *Dorothy* in the 1870s to race against the South Company gig in the Aldeburgh Regatta.

The pilots were the top regular earners in the beach community until 1899 when Trinity House ruled that all pilots for the North Channels into the Thames Estuary had to be based at Harwich. The Aldeburgh pilot companies were wound up, but their Look Outs were kept for meeting places.

The beach company at Aldeburgh was separate to the pilots and had their own hut on the beach in front of the town. However when a vessel was in danger any available man went off in the yawls. The beachmen fished, worked on pilot boats, salvaged or undertook what ever

The *Rachael Linda* was the last wooden boat working off Aldeburgh Beach, 2012.

The IH85, *Jim & Clare* and LT 468 at the north end of Aldeburgh beach, May 23 1994. The last generation of wooden boats were powerful and beamy; they needed to be to land on the open beach. When *Ocean Pride* was caught in a gale in 1972 she was smashed up on the shingle ridge just off the beach, but owner Sid Strowger got ashore unharmed and walked up the beach carrying a thwart.

'Deano' Fryer's *Jill Anne* returning from longlining off Slaughden in about 1990.

work they could get.

The gentry were already building large houses for summer visits and there was a drive to increase their number. In the 1890s the landowner Leveson Vernon Wentworth decided that the people living in makeshift shelters on Aldeburgh beach lowered the tone of the rising genteel holiday resort. As Lord of the Manor he owned the beach and sent the bailiffs and police in to clear the squatters off.

A battle lasted for several days and the beach squatters fought back by taking Wentworth's solicitor hostage and threatened to throw him into the sea. More police were brought in and the men fought with weapons made from fishing gear. Eventually the beach dwellers were driven off the beach and their huts and shelters pulled down.

For the fishing community the emphasis became selling more sprat and herring. There had been an ancient autumn fish dinner held in Aldeburgh, and in the Edwardian era so many sprat were being landed that they promoted the Sprat Dinner, modelled on the Colchester Oyster Festival, to encourage sales and these were held until 1906.

The Aldeburgh author George Goldsmith Carter recorded the risks that the fishermen took in their small open boats. If the wind suddenly increased, as it sometimes did, they had to abandon all their fishing gear at sea and flee for the beach at speed, either under sail or oar. Then they had to risk going through the breaking waves, knowing that the boat could be flung over and smashed to pieces at any moment.

As a young man Goldsmith Carter longed to go to sea and the great day came when he was asked to crew on the Aldeburgh 'booat' *Toddy* with Arny, the landlord of the 'Black Horse.' They left the beach when it was still dark and rowed for the whole trip. Aldeburgh men used to row offshore until they could see the Southwold lighthouse and then shoot their nets for sprat.

There was an unwritten rule never to 'wipe up' another boat by shooting nets too close and taking all the fish. If this happened and one boat got nothing for a night's work there was likely to be a fight on the beach when they came ashore.

Goldsmith Carter said they rowed ashore at dawn and walked home for breakfast. They sorted the nets out later by shaking the fish out onto the beach. The nets were then stowed neatly in the open 'net room' at the stern of the boat ready for the following night's fishing. When trawling, the fish were kept in the 'fish rooms,' boarded compartments amidships. When engines first came in the Aldeburgh men used to take them out during the herring season so as not to 'taint the fish.'

The fishing families in Aldeburgh were Cable, Burrell and Collis. The first Collis was an Irishman and his grandson Albert 'Alb' Collis ran a pleasure business in the summer with bathing huts. He had built the gaff boats *Swallow* and *Martin* for running pleasure trips in the summer. He also had a raft moored off the beach for swimmers. During World War II soldiers swam out to the raft and all put their weight on one side and broke it. Poor 'Alb' was watching from the shore and was so upset he had a heart attack and died.

Aldeburgh fishermen were having difficulty selling their catches, but they were reluctant to co-operate until the local residents helped them in 1921 to form the Aldeburgh Fishermen's Trade Guild. Over the next forty years the Guild played an important part in promoting the local fishing industry. Where the Aldeburgh Boatyard now stands, the Guild had a smokehouse and warehouses where sprat were salted and packed into tubs. In 1946 the Guild bought a large smokehouse in Oakley Square and they also had a shed where a cart was kept for transporting fish to the railway station.

Billy Burrell started fishing off the beach in 1938 as 'deck hand' with Tom Parnell. Billy Burrell remembered that just after World War II the Guild was sometimes sending two railway truckloads of fish to Billingsgate Market in a

The 22.9ft *Sheree Anne* launching off Aldeburgh beach in 2008.

Cod, skate and sprat on *Our Boys*, The catch off the Suffolk coast.

The *Content* and *Silver Jubilee* near South Lookout on Aldeburgh Beach in 2013 after eight boats had been repainted.

Alan Burrell repainting his boat *Content* on Aldeburgh beach, 2013.

The 2013 stage set for the opera 'Peter Grimes on the Beach' at Aldeburgh.

The Thorpe boats on the beach in about 1908.

Aldeburgh from Thorpeness.

day. Later the Guild hired lorries to take fish to the Lowestoft fish market and on a good day in the 1970s, lines of Bedford vans used to wait on Crag Path ready to take fish away.

The sailing boats had low sides for rowing, but when engines were fitted the power of the propeller pulled the hulls down into the water so that an extra plank, known as 'rose on' had to be added on to the hull sides. In the years after World War II there was a food shortage and a shortage of building timber. New, smaller fishing boats were built at Woodbridge with higher sides and sternposts cut for the propellers to fit under their sterns. Eversons built the 14ft *Sea Gull* to fish from Sizewell and in 1947 Whisstocks built the 12ft *Two Gals*. The 15ft *Suffolk Lad*, built for Billy Burrell by Frank Knights had an extra plank added when she was moved to fish from Sizewell. Aldeburgh fishermen worked these boats close inshore, on the grounds known as 'The Garden'.

In 1959, when Dr Janet Tait moved to Aldeburgh, there were thirty-eight boats on the beach and that number remained for about ten years. Fishermen had mostly lived in streets a few minutes walk from the beach, and kept their fishing gear at the back of their cottages, but as an increasing number of Londoners came down and bought up cottages forcing up house prices so that the fishermen had to move inland. Just after World War II the fishermen started putting up sheds on the beach as gear stores. The public came to buy fresh fish straight from the boats that had just landed. At that time fishermen were landing good catches, making a good income and ordering new boats.

The boats were all built by eye without plans. Fishermen used to go and see Frank Knights at the Ferry Quay, Woodbridge and mark out a rough plan of the boat on the floor. Frank was a very likeable and friendly man, but the actual boat building was done by his partner Phillip Gooch and other shipwrights. Because space was limited some boats were built in the second storey of the eighteenth century brick warehouses on the Ferry Dock although getting

the boats down from the second storey must have been a struggle. Part of this was later converted into Frank's flat.

At Waldringfield Ernie Nunn also built new boats for Aldeburgh beach. When this yard was bought by the Browns in 1975 there was still a contract to build three more new boats. Browns built the first two, but as they lost £1000 they kept the third boat, *Enterprise*, for their yard hack boat.

Shipwrights Trevor Moore and John White built open Suffolk clinker boats at the Fox's Felixstowe Ferry yard. The boats built for Dunwich beach were higher sided than those working from the Deben mouth. Felixstowe Ferry's last new wooden boat was the *Ellen* built in 1989 and John White, the Harbour Master, still uses her.

In 1986 Jim Churchyard told me, at his shed near the South Lookout how he had started fishing in the 18ft boat *Happy Thought* that still carried sails. The only other boat on Aldeburgh beach still carrying sails then was the *Two Gals*, because she had a low powered engine. It appears that the *Happy Thought*, like the *Ossie*, sank off Aldeburgh, but in both cases other boats rescued the crew.

Jim Churchyard said trawling in these low powered boats was quite difficult because their sterns kept lifting out of the sea. In the 18ft *Pauline* Jim had a quarter of a ton of shingle in bags in the stern to stop the trawl being lifted off the bottom. He also set the mizzen to keep the bow up into the wind. The trawl was 'shot' into the sea on the windward side so that the boat blew away from it and was then towed with two warps on the leeward side.

In about 1969, 'Mick the Brick' Wilkinson became skipper of the Maldon coaster *Kylix*. His first passage north was at night and he suddenly found himself in amongst about fifteen little white Aldeburgh boats with their mizzens set, outside the Aldeburgh Naps.

'What the hell are you all doing out here?' shouted Mick and back out of the darkness came a Suffolk voice shouting: 'trawling-bugger off!' The *Kylix* continued on to load shingle dredged off the Southwold Bar.

These little open beamy boats had a reputation for riding the seas like seagulls, but they still had to ride through breaking water to reach the safety of the beach. Being swamped was looked on as being 'bad seamanship,' but everyone rushed to assist a boat in trouble. It might be them next time. On one occasion a boat rolled over and the men on the beach used an axe to cut a hole in the bottom of the boat to get the crew out. Another time it took fourteen men to lift a boat back that had rolled over. After this some boats had steel 'roll bars' fitted just above the engine. These were also handy for putting a derrick on to lift the gear.

The *C & R* was built for Billy Burrell, named after his children Christine and Richard, and was once swamped when coming ashore on the 'White Lion' end of the beach. She was then owned by Pete Benstead, who was washed out of the *C & R* on to the beach face downwards and couldn't get up in his heavy boots and oilskins. Jim Churchyard ran down the beach into the water, grabbed his hood and dragged him up the beach away from the next breaking wave.

In about 1975 Pete bought his first boat, fitted a new £3,000 engine and earned the money back in three months by longlining for cod, well offshore. The 1970s are now regarded as being the period when Aldeburgh beach was a 'gold mine.' Billy Burrell's shed was at the north end of the beach and he had four boats going off at intervals so that they returned about every two hours, when the catch from the previous boat had been sold. The two men on each boat used to sell their catch direct to the public who knew they were getting fresh fish from the men who caught them. When the coaches came down to sea front they often left with everyone clutching a parcel of fish.

Billy kept his boats for eight years and used to order a new boat every two years; this kept maintenance costs down. He began to run out of names and it appears that he called his last boat *Babs*. Billy's son Richard Burrell began fishing

off Aldeburgh beach, but when he started on his own account, with a fibreglass boat, Billy suggested that he should work it off Thorpeness Beach. Richard worked the low-sided fibreglass skiff *Lollypop* and then the *Annabel* from here and later, when he moved to live in Leiston, began trammel netting, potting and longlining with the *Avril Rose*, out of Southwold.

Another man who left Aldeburgh beach to fish from a deep-water port was Terry Wightman. Terry's great-great grandfather had been drowned when his boat capsized whilst sprat fishing in Aldeburgh Bay. The cottage owner demanded that to help pay the rent the widow's thirteen year old son, John Orvis, must go away cod fishing on his Aldeburgh smack *Lady Montefiore* in the North Sea. John Orvis was very homesick and began to cry. The hard old fishermen tied a rope around him and threw him overboard. After they had pulled him back aboard they said that if he carried on crying they would throw him overboard without the rope next time. John Orvis managed to survive the harsh life in the Aldeburgh cod smacks and later became a beach fisherman and sometimes in the summer went crewing on King Edward VII's yacht.

Although Terry Wightman had strong family connections with Aldeburgh beach, he started off trawling around Havergate Island with Vic Brinkley's *Just the Job* which had a 4hp, Stuart Turner petrol engine. After that he bought the 16ft *Southern Cross* with an 8hp Stuart Turner engine and fished off Sizewell. At that time Jack Fryer and Joss Warner, with the *Newer*, were the only other fishermen working boats full time off Sizewell.

As the moving shingle at Sizewell created banks off the beach, making it difficult to land, Terry Wightman moved his boat to Aldeburgh. Terry's first new boat built by Overy at Lowestoft in 1962 was the *Viking* which had an 8hp Stuart Turner engine. Most new boats then cost about £450 but the *Viking* cost £850 and at the time was the most expensive beach boat built.

Terry's next boat, the *Gannet*, also had an 8hp

Stuart Turner. Terry decided he wanted a 28ft boat so that he could have a wheelhouse and radar. He asked Frank Knights to build him a new boat, but Frank said his shed was only big enough for a 21ft, so he settled for that. When he went to see the new boat, *Day Breeze,* he discovered the hull was only 17.6ft! Frank said that he couldn't find any wood long enough. Sadly there was no room for a wheelhouse.

The fishing was so good at this time that the boats sometimes came back to unload two or three times a day. Terry wanted a boat that could be beached easily and get off again quickly so he had the *East Wind* built at Lowestoft to a new design. The shape of the keel rose sharply at both ends to make beaching easier.

As the method of selling fish changed the fishermen abandoned the Fishermen's Guild and concentrated on selling their fish straight to the public. As Terry just liked being out fishing and disliked dealing with the public, an 'old man,' 'Zembuck' Ward, used to man his shed ashore. In 1970 Terry changed to working a decked craft from Lowestoft and became the top 'Dogger' in the North Sea, landing more dogfish than any other boat. He learnt their habits and followed them round the North Sea.

The problem with petrol engines was that they could not be started on the beach because they were water cooled and sucked in sand. At Aldeburgh the beachmen at the north end used to all gather to push Billy Burrell's boat off the beach with a 'sett' pole. In theory they pushed him through a calm patch, but for a bit of a laugh the men sometimes waited until there was a big wave and happily pushed Billy out to get wet. Once afloat Billy was able to start his engine and then tow the next boat off the beach and that, in its turn, pulled another boat off.

Jim Churchyard remembered that in about 1969 a whirlwind swept along the coast, one summers day, when all the boats were at sea. The lifeboat put to sea at once, but they found one boat happily trawling a mile and a half offshore, totally under aware of the whirlwind. When the boats were at sea in April 1972 it was far worse. A sudden ESE gale swept in and the lifeboat went out to escort them back to the beach. However Sid Strowger had been longlining in *Ocean Pride* at Hollesley Bay and when the lifeboat found them they were still fighting their way back. Fortunately the lifeboat men had passed lifejackets over to the three men in *Ocean Pride* before she was swamped on the shoal off the beach. The lifeboat managed to save the men before the boat was swept away. The *Ocean Pride* was swept north round the Ness and the next morning Sizewell men found her battered hull on their beach.

At about this time I was talking to Frank Knights at Woodbridge and noticed a transom of an Aldeburgh boat leaning against the wall. 'Oh' said Frank 'that boat broke up coming ashore and they brought the transom back for us to rebuild her!'

The arrival of powerful air-cooled Lister diesel engines was a tremendous boost to inshore fishing because they could be started while the boat was still ashore. With powerful engines they no longer had to have fine lined boats. The shipwright, Philip Gooch said the Aldeburgh men used to call the design of the new beamy type of boat 'bulldog bowed.'

The boats with their powerful diesel engines were able to go further out to sea. John Harling remembered going out eight miles to near the Shipwash in the 20ft *Enterprise* to longline for cod. Before hauling they used to go aboard the Shipwash lightship and exchange their newspapers for hot cups of tea with condensed milk. However John used to feel seasick in the slow rolling lightship and was always glad to get back to the quick motion of the *Enterprise.*

Many wooden boats were built for a particular type of fishing. The 19ft 2' x 8ft 10' *Our Boys* was built by Ernie Nunn at Waldringfield in 1976 for Billy Burrell. Billy moved the moulds out further when she was being built to make her beamy enough to work twenty-five sprat nets. Most of the beam was aft where the nets were stored with the result that the boat had a lot of buoyancy aft. The first 30hp Lister engine was

A visitor running down with the line to the winch as the *Lizzie* returns to Thorpe in about 1910. The *Lizzie* had probably been shrimp trawling as it has a tall mast and a large summer sail.

fitted amidships but this caused her to bury her bows at sea. To correct this problem a lighter air cooled engine was fitted further aft. In 1988 Kirk Stribling bought *Our Boys*, but as he found that working an air-cooled engine eight hours day was very noisy he fitted a water-cooled Lister.

Billy Burrell told me that the Aldeburgh custom of painting the top hull planks red or blue on a white hull came from the fishermen's habit of dropping into the lifeboat shed to see if there was any 'paint left over in the bottom of a tin.'

In the eighteenth century the Hunt family were building wooden vessels at Slaughden Quay and William Hunt sold the yard in 1880. H.W. Tilberry ran Hunt's yard for a while after this and then Allen built some small wooden boats there. There was a long gap in wooden boat building here until Russell Upson revived it when he bought the Slaughden yard in 1973. Russell, who had been Claude Whisstock's foreman at Woodbridge, remembered that the first boat he built at Slaughden was the 22ft *Charlotte E* for Eddie Strowger in 1973. Like

the other builders he didn't use plans or keep records of the boats he built. These beamy clinker hulled boats with powerful engines still had flat bottoms for landing through the surf.

When I talked to the Upsons in 1990 they were building a 22ft wooden boat for David Crips of Walberswick, and after this the roomy *Sea Spray* for Eddie Strowger. This appears to have been their last wooden beach boat built here, but it certainly was not the last wooden hull built by Upsons.

In 1998 the Welsh National Opera produced 'Peter Grimes' and Bryan Upson built two small Aldeburgh beach boats for this, one of which was rowed in the river before it went to Cardiff. In 2014 Upsons built the *Jay* and two other new rowing skiffs for Thorpeness Mere. The *Jay* was built for a resident as a memorial because he wished to create something more useful than a bench. At the time they were also building a Loch Long class day sailing racer.

Fibreglass hulls first appeared on the Suffolk coast in the early 1960s but regular wooden boat building continued. The wooden boats had a basket like quality and 'gave' when they

The central hut on Thorpe beach in about 1904 was the Fishermen's Shelter. A fisherman is watching the boats at sea and behind him is a net barrow and lobster pot.

pounded on the beach. Fishermen were not certain that the early fibreglass hulls were strong enough to take this pounding. However wooden boats had to be painted every year and they were beginning to think that love was poured into a wooden boat without it being returned.

Bryan Upson was the only builder to develop the traditional beach boats into a fibreglass version. He built about nine including *Ruben William*, with a wheelhouse, for fishing from Aldeburgh in 2006. The *Joseph William (III)* built for Sizewell in 2008 has been kept as an open boat to reduce the motion.

Dean 'Deano' Fryer's *Spring Tide* is a conventional fibreglass hull fitted with wooden skegs to keep her upright on the beach. As a boy Deano had gone down to watch and help unload the boats and in 1980 he started fishing off Aldeburgh beach. When he started there were twenty-four boats being launched into the darkness to go fishing. There was a policy to reduce the national fishing fleet and by 1995 the number working on Aldeburgh beach was down to eight.

Deano worked the wooden Aldeburgh boat

*Jill Anne* and moved on to own the *Enterprise* built by Frank Knights at Woodbridge. The wooden beach boats only made about 6 knots, but in 1995 Deano bought the *Excel*, a catamaran capable of 21 knots which completely changed his way of fishing. This catamaran had to be launched off the beach from a trailer pulled by a caterpillar tractor but their speed allowed them to do two types of fishing in one day.

The fishermen nearly always had a man ashore, often father or grandfather, to help out with landing and hauling up the beach. Dean had a 'flauterer' (helper), Mick Wilson who baited lines and sold fish ashore. They used to catch sprat as bait for the cod longlines, but later on used Falkland Island squid.

Deano gave up the catamaran because the powerful outboard on the stern, along with nets and other gear, were stolen from the beach. In 2009 Deano bought the monohull *Spring Tide* with an inboard engine and in 2013 he and crewman Paul 'Pixi' Gittins fished regularly from the beach.

Sometimes boats were worked single handed because they had power winches for hauling,

Thorpe Fishing Boat Sailing Match, in 1911. A huge crowd had gathered to watch the race start, entertained by a band.

but many fishermen have tales of getting into trouble when they are on their own. At least one man fell overboard but fortunately was able to climb back up the trawl warps with the boat still going along. Once when Colin 'Tootsie' Smith was working on his own, hauling crab pots about two miles offshore he caught his hand in a power winch, but managed to get it free.

In 2002 there were seven boats working on the beach, but Aldeburgh longshore fishing fleet almost faded out in the winter of 2005 when only two boats were fishing. Then in 2006 Alan Wood started working from the beach near the North Lookout again with the new fibreglass *Ruben William*. On the north end of the beach Kirk Strickling also bought new boat, the red catamaran *Enterprise*.

A fishing business on Aldeburgh beach requires a fibreglass hull, powerful engines, launching trailer and a tractor to clear the shingle. The old sailing boats with their wooden capstans had required little capital. Just plain hard physical work would have earnt men a living. Even in 1960 a new 18ft boat with a Lister diesel cost £750, but by 2014 it might take over £100,000 to set up a fishing venture from a Suffolk beach.

Some former fishermen kept their wooden boats on the beach simply to retain their right to land and have a shed there. The *Silver Spray* lay on the beach so long that she had her fishing quota taken away. Her owner re-registered her at Milford Haven, knowing that a quota was still being issued there but the authorities later closed this loophole.

It is not surprising that Benjamin Britten's most popular opera 'Peter Grimes,' is a story about Aldeburgh and its fishing community because he was clearly fascinated by the beach. Britten went out in Billy Burrell's boat *Boy Billy* and maintained a long friendship with the Burrell family.

In 2013 the Aldeburgh Festival decided to stage Benjamin Britten's opera 'Peter Grimes' on the Aldeburgh beach in front of Oakley Square. The production of 'Peter Grimes on the Beach' focused world attention on Aldeburgh beach and thirteen scruffy old wooden fishing boats were smartened up for the occasion.

Nicolas Hill, an interior designer, was captivated by the shape of the boats on the beach and started a campaign to raise money to conserve the redundant boats, hopefully to lead on to a programme of keeping them safe as part of Aldeburgh's character. In 2013 the Fishing Boat Conservation Fund raised £10,000, and Alan Burrell, a former fisherman, was hired to patch up and paint the dilapidated beach boats. As the *C & R* had already been painted, Alan started painting his own boat *Content*, a high-sided boat built in 1971. He went on to paint *Viking, Charlotte E, Silver Spray. Jill Anne, Silver Jubilee* and *One More*.

Some of these boats were hired by the Aldeburgh Festival to be part of the stage set for 'Peter Grimes on the Beach'. Fortunately the weather was kind to Aldeburgh Festival and this production of 'Peter Grimes' was acclaimed a great success.

The Aldeburgh fleet survives because is has a reasonable beach to land on and fresh fish can be retailed straight from the sheds. The last wooden boat on the beach in working order is 'Tootsie' Smith's *Rachel Linda*, named after his daughter and built in Russell Upson's Old Shed at Slaughden in 1978. His nephew Mark Freeman started fishing with him, but later bought his own catamaran *Roddy* to fish from further along the beach.

In 2015 two boats worked part time while three boats were fishing regularly from Aldeburgh beach. Refrigerators were fitted in the sheds and retailing fresh fish from the sheds had become very important. Kirk Strickling was smoking and retailing fish and another business in a shed was just selling fish they had smoked. Another new business in an Aldeburgh beach shed began retailing gear for anglers and the town's beach remains a small-scale commercial fishing centre.

## Thorpeness

In the nineteenth century the hamlet of Thorpe had about thirty cottages and a row of Coastguard cottages dotted about in the sand dunes. There were no trees or streets. In the 1830s the carpenter Joshua Chard settled in Thorpe and when he had no work ashore he acted as a bumboatman, sailing out to passing ships and selling food. He bought a fast Cornish lugger, which had been seized for smuggling, and ran his own beach company. Half the salvage money went to the crew and half to Chard and his lugger. Chard was called the 'Suffolk Hero' in local newspapers because he was very keen on saving lives. In 1870, he had the 28ft boat *Rescue* built by William Hunt at Slaughden with money raised by the public. Chard also acted as an unofficial pilot and was engaged in this work when he drowned in 1875, aged 63.

The original settlement of Thorpe had been on the Ness near the mouth of Thorpe Haven, the shallow outlet for the Hundred River. As the sea moved inland there was a constant battle to keep Thorpe Haven open to let the fresh water escape. Percy Westrup, born in 1888, recorded that his grandfather had told him that the Dutch palingaken used to come in here to shelter in bad weather when sailing to Billingsgate with live eels in their wet wells. One of the Dutch boats got stuck in the Haven and had to jettison its eels before it could get out. According to Percy Westrup's grandfather, this was the reason that there were so many eels in the Haven marshes.

Every time a gale closed off the Haven mouth about thirty men used to dig the shingle out creating a new channel to let the fresh water escape. In about 1905 there was still enough water in the channel for young Percy and his friends to take a boat into the Haven and go net fishing in the marsh ditches. In the end the channel completely silted up and was replaced by the sluice.

Grandfather Westrup also recalled that the smugglers were landing tobacco, whisky and rum one night, when they saw the Coastguard man patrolling along the beach. One of the smugglers jumped out of the boat, up to his neck, got ashore and shouted 'for God sake run back to Thorpe and get some help as our boat is full of water and nets.' The Coastguard ran back to Thorpe and while he was gone they got the contraband ashore. When the rescue party came back the boat was up high and dry and

to Bawdsey beach, for six weeks in May, to go lobstering near the Cutler Bank. They used to leave at about 5am with father sailing the big boat towing the smallest boat while son, Percy Westrup, sailed the middle-sized boat.

They used to haul the largest boat ashore, at East Lane, Bawdsey, turn it over and cover it up with a sail. This was where they slept and ate. The middle-sized boat was used to work the hoop nets and they sailed to Harwich in their small boat to sell lobsters and a few crabs. At weekends they sailed up to Slaughden and walked back to Thorpe.

The Felixstowe Ferry men greatly disliked the Thorpe men working the grounds off East Lane, but the practice ended after these open boats were caught in bad weather rounding Orfordness and the Westrups only just made it into Orford Harbour at Shingle Street.

Henry Harling's 18ft boat *Industry* returning to Thorpe. The foresail sheet is taking the strain over the aft leeward thole, while Percy Westrup gets ready to jump out and haul her up the beach.

the crew said they had managed to bail the boat out.

There were so many shipwrecks on Thorpe Ness that the estate owner, Ogilvie, was appalled by the loss of life. He financed and built the Wreck House with a watchtower on the Ness. This had a store of food, blankets and first aid equipment and was manned in bad weather. When a ship went ashore, a bell was rung to summoned help from Thorpe and Sizewell. Sadly the Wreck House seems to have been used as a mortuary more than anything else.

In about 1908, the Westrups used to take their three boats eighteen miles down the coast

On another occasion Fred and Dick Wilson were coming ashore under sail at Thorpe when a squall turned them right over. Two other fishermen came to their rescue and the boat drifted ashore.

In 1910 the London barrister Glencairn Stuart Ogilvie inherited the large Sizewell Estate and started to develop Thorpe as the summer holiday village of mock Tudor houses called Thorpeness. Ogilive's grand plan worked well and the local fishermen were given part time work. They looked after the boats on Thorpeness Mere and their wives took in washing and cleaned houses. By 1914 there were seven groups of boats working off the beach giving employment to fourteen fishermen.

Henry Harling's 22ft *Gypsy Queen* with ballast bags piled beside her on Thorpe Beach in about 1909.

Ogilvie became worried by the amount of erosion on the coast and made the tenants of his farm plant marram grass along the coast. This caught the sand blowing from the beach to build up dunes and seems to have worked well. In the 1953 Floods most of the boats were hauled up the beach to higher ground, but the sea broke through the dunes and one boat was swept on to the marshes behind.

Another problem at Thorpeness was that a shingle bank sometimes built up just off the beach preventing the men from launching their boats. Fishermen sometimes moved their boats to Sizewell for the sprat season where landing was easier. Generally speaking there was an unwritten rule that the men of Dunwich, Sizewell, Thorpe and Aldeburgh all fished in their own areas in front of their homes.

During World War I some of the 6th (Cyclist) Battalion of the Suffolk Regiment were billeted at Thorpe and they patrolled the coast watching out for a German invasion. The soldiers also fenced off the beaches with barbed wire, but left a 20ft gap for the fishermen to get through. One dark morning Percy Westrup and his

skipper Harry Ship were trawling about two miles off Aldeburgh when they noticed a boat approaching but suddenly realised it was a submarine.

The submarine came right up to them, shone a searchlight on them and an officer asked which town they were off. They shouted 'Aldeburgh!' and a voice politely replied 'thank you, thank you' as the submarine steamed away.

Percy said to his skipper 'did you see the number on the conning tower?'

'Yes' said his skipper 'it was E2, not a British number.' Once ashore they reported it to the Coastguard and later the German submarine was captured. The Thorpe Coastguard was awarded an OBE for this and the fishermen got a 'Thank you.'

Percy went on to crew with Henry Harling on the 22ft *Gypsy Queen*. Once they went trawling in Hollesley Bay when the wind dropped and they started rowing for home. They offered to give a passing motor coaster some fish in exchange for a tow up the coast, but the skipper just laughed and told them 'you should have started earlier!'

It was hard work rowing twelve miles

Thorpe Beach after a high tide.

Percy Westrup and Tim Brown had been trawling in *Three Sisters*, in about 1935.

Amos Cooper on his Girl *Elsie* on Thorpe beach in 1949. His wife used to go out with him to help with the bailing, as the boat used to leak. Once when coming ashore they dropped a herring into the water and Mrs Cooper jumped out and retrieved it. Amos was amazed at the effort made for just one herring.

Russell Middleditch and Richard Wilson gutting cod beside the *Happy Times* in about 1972.

Jonathan and Robert Simper getting a beam trawl aboard the *Pet* while trawling under sail, 1985.

standing up, beachmen style, looking forward, in a three-ton boat loaded with gear and fish. They arrived back at Thorpe at 12.30pm to find their families waiting on the beach with lanterns, very relieved to see them safely home.

If there was no wind, the boats were sometimes rowed up the coast, sprat nets shot and then they drifted back on the tide to the landing. Usually the sprat nets were shot at half ebb tide while herring nets were shot at half flood tide.

Henry Harling had been born in 1883 in a little brick cottage that his grandfather had built at Thorpe, and then lived in until he died in 1895. Henry had three boats for different types of fishing. He used the 22ft *Gypsy Queen* for trawling in the summer and often trawled down to the Sizewell bank. The Thorpe boats used to go down with the tide and race back. He used the 18ft *Industry* for herring drifting in the autumn and a smaller 15ft 'pot boat' for working in the summer for lobster 'on the Rocks', a rough area of seabed off Thorpe.

Another Thorpe fishermen 'Keydie' Wilson had gone to sea aged eleven, in the Aldeburgh cod smacks that went to the Icelandic fishery. The Aldeburgh smacks were actually based at Harwich and only returned home at the end of the season. Between voyages, the men used to walk home taking the ferries at Landguard, Bawdsey, Butley River and Slaughden. Keydie got his nickname because he once dived off a Harwich quay and rescued a boy. He became known as 'Quay Dive' and that, in fishermen's style, was corrupted into 'Keydie.'

When one of the Cables of Aldeburgh bought the new 'pot' boat 15ft *Pet* for working lobster pots Keydie helped him bring it back from Southwold. As they couldn't afford the sails and gear, they rowed her all the way back to Aldeburgh.

During World War I Percy Westrup had a permit to fish with his 15ft *Speedwell* as far away as Harwich but during World War II the Thorpeness men had to stay very close to the coast. In 1943 they had a record year for cod

The 18ft *Three Sisters* sailing with one reef down.

The *Three Sisters'* swivel hook, on the foresail sheet. When the foresail is reefed the hook is moved up to the next iron thimble on the cringle.

Loading the *Shady Nook*, the last of the Thorpe boats, onto the trailer. Robert Simper, Tony Ralph, Jonathan Simper and John Westrup. 2008.

One of the winches that replaced the bar capstans for hauling boats up the beach can be seen in front of the Thorpeness fisherman's sheds. The shed on the right belongs to John Westrup (formerly Percy Westrup's) then Richard 'Lobster' Wilson's shed, (formerly Amos Cooper's) and Tim Brown's on the lower end. There was a shed behind these, where blind Will Cook made baskets, after walking every day from Aldringham.

when they were shooting ten long lines, just north of the Ness. The fisherman had their own smokehouses for herring, but they usually sold their catch to fish merchants in Leiston and villages around there.

During World War II the army moved mines from the road to the beach, using a narrow gauge railway. After this the fishermen used the railway track to move herring up to the road, where the Aldeburgh Guild lorry collected them. The boys had a good time riding on the truck, which with an extra push, came off the rails and went right across the road.

Fishermen seldom used the names of their boats; instead they were known by the names of their skippers. In his memoirs Percy Westrup never gave the name of his boat, he just said that she was an 18ft all oak boat, built at Southwold in 1884, and in 1926 he had put the first engine in.

Percy Westrup and Tim Brown had the 18ft *Three Sisters* with an 8hp petrol Stuart Turner engine and were the last men fishing full time off Thorpeness. After Percy sold this boat Tim Brown ordered a 15.1ft x 6.8ft x 2.7ft boat

The Wreck House, on the Thorpe Ness, was intended to be a refuge for shipwrecked sailors.

'Booty and the Beast.' Mr H. Booty on Sizewell beach with an 8.6ft shark on a net barrow in 1911.

from Everson at Woodbridge in 1955 with an engine and a lugsail. Inspired by a popular song, she was named *Shady Nook*. Thorpeness men started to favour the smaller boats because of the difficulties of getting off their beach. On some occasions, when they were trying to get into the sea over a flat sandy beach in front of the shingle their boats were 'cast,' knocked sideways back up the beach, and they couldn't get off.

It is said that Tim Brown never went outside the Aldeburgh Napes, about four miles out, in the *Shady Nook*. Later the fisherman had powerful engines and laughed about the 15ft *Shady Nook* staying inshore, but with only an 8hp petrol Stuart Turner engine a sudden head sea could have been more than she could cope with.

John Westrup is proud of having started fishing 'under sail,' because as a boy, in about 1956, he used to go out with George Wilson in the *Pet*, under sail, to lay lobster pots on The Rocks. In 1968 John Westrup and Tony Ralph

bought the *Shady Nook*. They had other jobs ashore, but came from fishing families and used to work the little boat part time.

The Fishermen's Shelter on sand dunes had been the centre of Thorpe fishing but as the holiday bungalows increased this was removed. The fishermen's sheds had been dotted about near their capstans and boats but these were moved to a group behind the sand dunes. In 1970 the estate owner Mrs Wentworth decided that the fishermen were untidy and ordered them off her beach. They all moved further north and early one morning; Richard 'Lobster' Wilson's hut was moved up the road on rollers.

There was great activity on Thorpeness beach during the winter weekends when the *Shady Nook* and Russell Middleditch's 16ft *Happy Times* landed cod. In the summer they used to go crabbing and shrimp trawling on Saturday and Sunday mornings. The catch was then boiled in front of the sheds and local people came down to buy them.

The returns from fishing got smaller and the *Shady Nook* was used less, until John's son Graham became keen on fishing and they used to go herring drifting again. In 2005 the *Shady Nook* was way offshore when she started to leak badly and after this the Westrups bought the 20ft fibreglass boat *Gill-Jan*. At that time the beach had become very steep and they had a terrible time getting her into the water. In 2008 they moved *Gill-Jan* to Southwold Harbour.

In 1981 my son Jonathan and I visited Thorpeness beach looking for a boat to restore, and found Richard Wilson's 15ft 'pot boat' *Pet* in a poor state. When we asked about her future we were told that she would probably go on a November fifth bonfire. When we asked if we could buy her, we were told that she was a very good boat and would soon be fitted out for fishing again. We did buy the *Pet* and the elderly Tim Brown came out of his bungalow to see the old boat being loaded on to Frank Knights' trailer to be taken to Woodbridge for a rebuild.

The first day we sailed the *Pet* with a dipping lug foresail I was totally unable to control her. Later that summer I went up to Southwold and the retired fisherman 'Ernie' Standard asked 'Are you the people who have done up one of our boats? Well you are doing it all wrong!' Ernie burrowed under his shed, where all the sailing punt gear had been carefully stored for decades and showed us how the gear worked. After that things fell into place. In the autumn we went herring drifting, and suddenly realised that everything about this Suffolk beach boat made sense.

Later, we found the hulk of another sailing beach boat, *Three Sisters*, in Ralph Brinkley's yard at Orford. Some time before she had had problems with her stern leaking. Frank Knights and Keith Cutmore went over and suggested to Ralph that the cheapest form of repair was put a cement box over the leaks in the stern. Ralph was a man who knew his own mind and refused to have a cement box in his boat. Frank took Ralph up to the 'Jolly Sailor' for a drink while Keith quietly put a cement box in the boat's stern and stopped all the leaks.

When we found the *Three Sisters* in 1981 in Orford she was an abandoned wreck in the corner of Ralph's yard. I was very keen to have a local boat restored, but Ralph wouldn't sell me the old boat and it took about three years before he agreed that if I bought the Stuart Turner petrol engine he would give me the hulk.

Like most of the sailing Suffolk boats, the *Three Sisters* had been built of oak planks on oak frames, but after years of being hauled ashore none of the planks were worth saving. Instead Chris Murphy supplied thirty-five cubic feet of larch from his sawmill at Sudbourne. This had come from 120-year old tree, blown over in North Norfolk. We retained the fittings, some knees and most importantly, the hull shape of the original boat. At Knights', John Russell White was in charge of the rebuild and said in horror, 'You do realized that this 18ft hull has got thirty-six knees!' I replied that she must still keep thirty-six knees because she obviously needed them.

The major alteration was placing the propeller under the stern. This spoilt her sailing ability, because the keel lost its grip on the water, but for leisure boating a 13hp diesel engine made sense. Also the old sailing hull was a plank lower, because in the old days they spent a lot of time rowing. However the extra plank was needed because an engine pulls the hull down into the water, particularly at the stern.

We based the *Three Sisters'* sails on the 1911 photograph of the *Lizzie* coming ashore with a shrimp trawl at Thorpe. She had her tall 'summer gear' in her that included a large mizzen. However I found the large mizzen made far to much 'weather helm,' and pushed her up into the wind but with a smaller mizzen she handles much better.

Billy Burrell told me that the *Three Sisters* had been the 'fastest boat at Aldeburgh and Thorpe and at the regatta races she used to be hauled back up the beach before the other boats finished.' The *Three Sisters* is beamy in the bows and this used to help lift her as soon as she hit the wave when going off a beach. No doubt her speed had come from being narrow aft. While based in the River Deben we have cruised the coast between Maldon and Lowestoft. *Three*

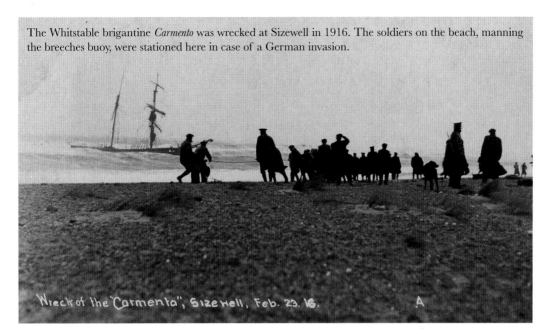

The Whitstable brigantine *Carmento* was wrecked at Sizewell in 1916. The soldiers on the beach, manning the breeches buoy, were stationed here in case of a German invasion.

Wreck of the "Carmenta", Sizewell, Feb. 23. 16.

*Sisters* rides the waves like a little duck, and her gear, laid out for men to handle in the dark, is very simple. Two of us can handle her under sail and we have relearned the lost art of handling a sailing beach boat, which has brought us a great deal of pleasure.

## Sizewell Gap

The loss of the town and harbour of Dunwich, which vanished under the sea, is well recorded. The erosion at Sizewell may not have been on the same scale and is almost unrecorded, but the old village does appear to have gone under the waves of the cold North Sea.

In medieval times Sizewell may have been a settlement beside a small inlet. It was part of the Leiston Abbey Estate and in 1232 Sizewell was granted its own market, which is likely to have been an outlet for the fish landed here. In about 1600 the sea moved inland so that most of medieval Sizewell vanished.

A glimpse of medieval Sizewell came when a cable route was being constructed to take the power from the Greater Gabbard Offshore Windfarm inland. Part of the old settlement, in front of the 'Vulcan' public house, was excavated in 2008 and a well with the sides lined with the remains of a 6m clinker built, iron fastened boat was discovered, dating from about 1300.

This is the earliest known beach boat from the Suffolk coast, apart from the Anglo Saxon longships excavated at Snape and Sutton Hoo. The Sizewell boat was built in a similar way to the Sutton Hoo ship and in the six hundred years between them not much had changed. To stop the gaps of the Sizewell boat leaking between the overlapping planks she had been 'luted' with animal hair mixed with tar. As boat builders' tools improved this practice was abandoned, but the basic method of construction remained much the same right up to the early 1990s when wooden boat building for longshore fishing boats ceased.

In the eighteenth century the lonely Sizewell Gap was a favourite place for the armed smuggling gangs. They took trains of pack animals inland from here, loaded with tobacco and brandy. The gangs were feared and usually went unopposed. The Hadleigh Gang operated from Sizewell Gap and there is an eighteenth century account, of 300 horses and 100 carts waiting on Sizewell beach to unload a 'crop' of tea. Smuggling was then big business and highly organised.

Noel Cattermole's longshore boat *Joseph William*, at Sizewell. Southwold is nine miles away on the other side of the bay and Covehithe beyond. In the medieval period all the sea in this view would have been land.

The *Joseph William* being hauled off
Sizewell Beach, 2014.

Noel and Peter emptying lobster pots on the Rocks off Thorpeness in *Joseph William*.

A 10lb bass in *Joseph William's* trammel net off Minsmere Haven, 2014.

Gulls taking a rest from scavenging, while the trammel nets are being hauled aft on the *Joseph William*.

The smuggler's favourite type of sailing vessel was the lugger because the halliards had several purchases to keep the leading edge of the flax sails tight. This allowed the luggers to sail closer to windward. The gaff rig of the revenue cutter was a very versatile rig, but in a chase the luggers were able to out-sail them upwind.

Sizewell had its own lifeboat and lifeboat shed until 1853 when they were moved to Aldeburgh to start the station there. Sizewell and Dunwich just had 'pulling' (oared) lifeboats, which limited the area they could work in and they had problems finding enough able men to launch and man the boats.

The fishermen on the Suffolk coast were not worried about speed because they didn't go very far. Fishing boats, yawls and lifeboats used the lug because the sail could always be lowered quickly in a squall. Also, coming on to a beach or rounding up alongside a vessel in trouble the sail would come down at once when the halliards were released. In an open lugger the foresail sheet was NEVER made fast, but was sometimes put round a thole on the leeward side, to take the strain. The yawls had a post amidships to take the strain of the foresheet.

Another advantage of lug rig in an open boat was that it gave maximum space to work. When working the fishing gear the sail could be lowered and stowed on one side. While hauling pots the men rowed, standing up facing forward so that they could see the next pot. Because they landed on beaches the East Anglian luggers didn't have a keel or centreboard. To go to windward, they used to put an oar over the leeward side and pull the bow up into the wind or just lower the gear and row up into the wind. Their real secret of success was working the tides. They made sure that the tide was in their favour and went off the beach on one tack and came back on the other. The beach at Sizewell is a good landing place but is constantly moving, the southerly wind leaves sand and a northerly usually leaves shingle

In the late nineteenth century more holidaymakers came to the Sizewell area and a few fishing and tripper boats were kept on the beach. In most places the men owned their own capstans, but at Sizewell there appears to have been one capstan provided by the landowner. The capstan was still there in the 1960s and two men were able to pull a boat up with it, but it was easier with four men. The sail and oar Suffolk boats were lighter because they didn't have engines.

By the 1930s Sizewell had become a busy tourist centre and in the summer there was a regular bus service along a coastal track to a café at Minsmere Sluice. During World War II the army had a rifle range on the coast and the Minsmere track was closed. In fact, in preparation for a German invasion, the whole Suffolk coast became a military zone and was closed to the public. There were mines on the beach, miles of barbed-wire fencing and anti tank blocks near roads and on the beaches. For several miles inland it was a fortified area with pillar-boxes, gun emplacements and tank traps. There were also large numbers of troops stationed in camps ready to repel an invasion.

Early in World War II a German submarine sent an inflatable boat ashore at Sizewell at night and a bottle of German beer and a sailor's hat was left on the beach. This was intended to frighten the English into believing that there was soon going to be a German invasion leading to the conquest of the British Isles. This is the only known case of Germans landing on an East Anglian beach during World War II.

In 1941 thirty-two young Dutchmen decided to flee from their Nazi-occupied country and canoed across the North Sea from Katwijk to England. Sadly only eight of these Englandvaarders (England voyagers) made it across. The Brothers Henri and William Peteri managed to land at Sizewell. They were promptly arrested by the police and locked up, but Henri said he felt free for the first time.

In August 2011 Harry Franks organised eight canoes to re-enact this voyage across the North Sea. Most of the canoeists were taken aboard the support craft on the way, but three Dutch marine canoeists reached Sizewell. They were welcomed on the beach by Prince Harry and Olly Hicks, who had previously rowed solo across the Atlantic.

After World War II hand winches were used to pull the boats up but when the heavier motorboats appeared the winches were fitted with motors. The Sizewell men regarded themselves as being fishermen, but many gave up fishing during the winter to work in Garrett's ironworks at Leiston.

In the 1960s fishermen had five boats working full time and some part timers worked from Sizewell. The Aldeburgh Fisherman's Guild's lorry took all their fish to Lowestoft Fish Market. The men were often landing about half a ton of herring and these had to be boxed up and carried up the beach. When the fish were there they earned up to £3,000 on a good week (modern value now about £9,000) with an 18ft boat. Successful fishermen were having new boats built about every four years to replace those that had been strained when landing on the beach.

The boom years for longshore fishing boats at Aldeburgh, Sizewell and Dunwich were in the 1960-70s. There were plenty of fish, prices were high and there were no problems with quotas. These years coincided with the arrival of powerful diesel engines and larger boats with more beam, that were far better at sea.

There were not enough fishermen at Sizewell to sustain a boat builder, but an enterprise started in the 1950s by Major Abthorpe to give employment to Ukrainian refugees. As Major Abthorpe knew nothing about boat building he bought an old beach boat and asked the Ukrainian workers to copy it. This venture had the unusual name of Abthorpe Ukrainian Industries and was based in Waterloo Road in Leiston. The boats that Abthorpe Ukranian Industries built included the *Hope* and the 18ft x 7.6 ft *Griff LT50*, built in 1963. The *Griff* was built for the Davies brothers to fish off Sizewell beach, but they parted company and sold the boat. Fishermen said these boats didn't have a 'belly' (the full round bottom of the true beach boat) and when they were in breaking waves, on the beach, water slopped over the side.

When launching there was a real problem with the old wooden boats. To get through the breaking water the men sometimes had to push their boats at the stern with water coming over their thigh boots. Once afloat they often undressed, not a good idea on a cold dark winter's morning, and tried to ring the water out of their clothing. They often worked for the rest of day in damp clothes, both afloat and when sorting out their catch on the beach.

As men retired at Sizewell young men didn't fill their places and the boats were sold. The Davies sold the *Griff* to Southwold where it became the *Why Not*, and was sometimes used for fishing by Billy Stannard. In the 1970s she was given a new 10hp Sabb single cylinder water cooled diesel engine. When David Cleveland bought her in 2004 she had been used for pleasure and the owner had added his dog's names to make her *Why Not Archie Bear*. David based her at Manningtree and for eight happy years explored every inch of the River Stour and went netting for bass and mullet. As the boat was very stable she was just right for family and fishing trips, but she acquired a bad leak and was sold to Steve Buckle, who works for John Buckley at the Blackshore, Southwold.

The MMO Inspector discouraged wooden boats in the Suffolk inshore fishing because he realised that fishermen were no longer painting and maintaining their boats annually. Steel and fibreglass boats were easier for the fishermen to maintain.

One fine autumn day in 2013 I went down to Sizewell, hoping to get a photograph of the *Joseph William*, the only full time fishing boat at Sizewell, but I was too late, and the big blue boat was already hauled out of the water. As I walked back, I saw three men studying the back of my Landrover. I thought I was about to be told off for parking in the wrong place, but Noel Cattermole pointed at my beach boat logo on my tyre cover and said 'What's this- IH 81? I don't know that one'.

I explained that it was a sailing beach boat *Three Sisters* that I had had restored. At once we launched into a long conversation about Suffolk boats, several of which Noel had had built. When he left school in 1971 he started work with Jack Fryer, on the *Four Sisters*, built by Frank Knights in 1960 and fitted with a 13hp diesel Lister air cooled engine. Noel loved the

life and at the time the money was good. He then worked the *Two Jacks* for Jack Fryer and Jack Darkins. Noel first worked his own boat off the beach below Sizewell cliff and eventually ordered the boat *Jill Anne*, named after his sisters, from Ernie Nunn at Waldringfield. This boat cost £2,500 in 1975.

Noel's next new boat had been the *Sarah Amy*, named after one of his daughters. This boat had an unusual background. In April 1972 the Aldeburgh boats were caught at sea in a sudden Force 7 gale from the ESE, and the Lifeboat went out to escort them back. The last one, *Ocean Pride*, could not make it and they had to take the three men off just before she was dashed to pieces on the beach. Next morning the keel and other parts of this boat, all good wood, were washed up on Sizewell beach, where they were winched ashore. This wreck was taken to Frank Knights and he rebuilt her 'on spec'. Half way through the rebuild the shipwright working on her died and eventually the boat was completed and sold as the *Sarah Amy*. Noel's next boat was the 19.5ft *Joseph William*, built by Upsons at Slaughden Quay in 1988 for £9,015. Unfortunately Noel didn't like this boat because she was too fine forward and was 'dirty' (wet) at sea.

In about 1994 this boat was sold to Pete Benstead, a shipwright and fisherman at Orford. Noel bought a Cygnus fibreglass hull and Pete fitted this boat out. Noel used this *Joseph William* until 2006 when it was sold to a fisherman in Galway. At the time the European Union was giving grants to the Irish fishermen.

As Noel needed a boat that could cope with being swamped, he bought one of Upsons fibreglass hulls that they had developed in their own mould. This had incorporated the best hull shape of wooden boats and had a sealed deck and scuppers to let the water out. This new *Joseph William* has a watertight engine box so that the engine doesn't stop when coming through the breakers. It had taken many years of evolution and heartache to reach the design of the present *Joseph William*. Noel regards this as being the ultimate development of the Suffolk longshore beach-based boats.

The latest *Joseph William* is not turned round on the beach, but has a stern winch and a combination rope to a kedge anchor laid offshore so that she can be hauled out stern first. If she takes in water it runs out through the wash ports. There are several other boats kept and used from Sizewell Beach, mostly for shrimp trawling in the summer, but in 2014 Noel Cattermole and his crew Stephen Runnacles had become the only full time fishermen there. With a highly seaworthy fibreglass boat Noel and Stephen sometimes managed to go fishing for 340 days a year because this boat can be worked in anything up to a force 6.

One fine July morning I joined the *Joseph William* on one of her trips to sea. Going off a beach is a very sudden way of getting afloat. One moment you are on dry land and the next you are in the open sea. Once afloat the gulls came screeching overhead and then sat on the rail watching us with intent. I don't think that, if I had not been there, a word would have been exchanged between Noel and Stephen. They had worked out a routine so that both knew exactly what to do. When the lobster pots had been emptied and re-baited, Noel pointed to where the pots were to be re-anchored for another two days. These pots were on the top end of The Rocks, a patch of rough ground stretching from Thorpe Ness to Aldeburgh.

A trammel net was shot and left to drift on the tide and later hauled up near the power station outflow, while we motored up to anchored trammel nets off Minsmere. Here a seal soon appeared to watch the hauling. Noel believed that so many seals are being reared in seal sanctuaries that they have lost their fear of humans and look on men as a source of food. As it was neap tides, which are not very strong, most of the trammel nets were anchored close to shore, but in bad weather they would have been laid about a mile out to sea. On a spring tide, when the current is stronger, a drifting trammel has been more successful than trawling off Sizewell.

When the trammels came up from the bottom they were full of stones, some of which had been identified as French. The belief is that when the original Leiston Abbey was built, ships coming into Minsmere Haven were wrecked on the beach or it could have been that a ship was wrecked at the entrance, on a beach that is now well out to sea.

It was a wonderful summer's morning and during the hauling of the pots and nets we could clearly see the whole coastline from Aldeburgh to Southwold. There were a few yachts and a survey vessel in sight, but not a single fishing vessel. Noel said that, on a day like this, only twenty years before, the sea would have been dotted with white beach boats working the inshore waters. The *Joseph William* strayed into the Dunwich men's waters, but there were no boats on Dunwich beach so no one cared.

Once ashore, and hauled up the beach by a winch, the catch was loaded into the truck and taken back to Noel's house, just the other side of sand dunes. Noel had a saleroom on the side of his house and people soon started arriving to buy the fresh fish.

## DUNWICH

According to legend a forest once extended for miles in front of the medieval town of Dunwich. It was claimed that in 1884 a Southwold boat

Mark Myers' watercolour of the Dunwich lifeboat *Ann Ferguson* about to take fourteen men off the Finnish barque *Flora* off Sizewell Sluice in 1888. The barque had developed a bad leak in the North Sea and her master decided to beach her. The men were landed at Sizewell Gap and walked up to the 'Vulcan Arms' for food and a singsong.

Boats on Dunwich beach from *Three Sisters* on May 23 1994.

The *Alice Maud* at Dunwich, with All Saints Church in the background, in about 1905. The *Alice Maud* was built in 1884 and was used for fishing and pleasure trips. In 1957 she was working off Kessingland with an old 7hp car engine and had been 'rose on' with an extra side plank.

Mrs Brown, Dr Warwick and a begger man hauling a boat up Dunwich Beach in about 1905.

had trawled up Roman masonry three and half miles off the beach at Dunwich. It is believed that there was a Roman port beside the Dunwich River and Anglo-Saxons had a trading centre here that grew into the major Medieval port. Ships had sailed to the Icelandic cod fishery from here.

Dunwich had a wall to protect it from enemy attack, but the encroaching sea was a far greater problem. The people fought back against the sea by placing faggots along the foot of the cliff to break the relentless force of the waves but the sea kept nibbling away at the land. In 1328 the river entrance was blocked by a storm with a spit of shingle and sand and the river burst through about two miles to the north. The towns of Walberswick and Southwold were delighted with this because it brought trade to their quays. In 1331 Dunwich men fought back and started digging a new entrance, by hand, to bring ships back to their quays. To prevent this, sixteen men were sent in a boat from Walberswick to stop them digging and in the bitter fight that followed the Walberswick men were killed.

When the king assembled a fleet to attack Flanders in 1341 Dunwich sent nine ships and 263 men to join the expedition at Gosford (King's Fleet), Felixstowe. The sea continued to move inland mostly in bad storms and by 1540 it had reached the market place in the middle of town. In 1590 there was a long lawsuit with Walberswick over Dunwich's claim that they had the right to charge ships to enter the river. However the glory days were well and truly over. Most people realised that Dunwich was doomed and the major merchants moved away. The loss of Dunwich and its port affected the whole Suffolk coast and population dwindled.

With the people gone, this lonely coast was ideal for the eighteenth century smugglers. The Dunwich smuggler Isaac Larter used to hang a lantern in the ruined church on the cliff top when it was safe to land on the beach. This light couldn't be seen by customs men on the land but was visible from the sea.

A 1752 print shows Dunwich's new role as a beach landing. It shows a double-ended spritsail rigged boat just off the beach below the cliff and an unsigned mid-Victorian painting has black double-ended boats pulled up on a track in a cliff overlooking Dingle Marshes. An 1880

Jonathan Simper beside a Kessingland beach skiff on Dunwich beach in 1979. This type of rowing boat was used to work close inshore.

Longshore fishermen had a protest on Dunwich beach in 1983. Left to right. Clive Coates, Steve King, Ray Woodrow, Steve Collett and Barry Tibbenham.

They were worried about the quota system that they believed would lose them their jobs. In spite of this protest the last boat gave up working from Dunwich thirty years later.

The *Fred's Last* and the *Two Sheilas* at Dunwich in 1984 with Phillip Holmes, Steve Collett and Barry Tibbenham.

The *Fred's* Last being turned on a turntable at Dunwich ready to be relaunched bows first, in 1984. The engines made the boats too heavy to turn round by hand. By tradition the East Anglian boats were always turned on the beach clockwise. Older men had been superstitious and said that it was 'asking for trouble' to turn a boat 'against the sun'. More recently beachmen had decided that it was easier to turn their boats clockwise, as most people were right handed.

Dunwich beach in about 1996. In the twentieth century Dunwich had been at it height as an inshore fishing centre In about 1984 there were fourteen boats on the beach being used for full-time and part-time fishing.

'Dodger' Holmes, trawling in the *Dodger off* Dunwich, in 2001

oil painting by Thomas Smythe shows Dunwich beach with eight boats. This also shows that the landowner understood the problems of erosion, as there is a breakwater-groyne and a stout wooden barrier to stop the waves from eating the cliff away.

Every summer in the 1860-70s the 120 ton Southwold schooners *Woodland Lass* and *Hearts of Oak* used to discharge coal from Hartlepool onto the open beach at Dunwich. The cargoes were discharged as quickly as possible into carts and the horses had to wade up to their bellies to try to finish on one tide. Once discharged the schooners were hauled off to an anchor laid out astern.

In 1888, two years after the Dunwich Corporation had been abolished, the Dunwich lifeboat had its best-known rescue. This was when coxswain Isaac Dix, Dunwich sub-post master, went out in a gale to the barque *Flora* that was aground on Sizewell beach. He skilfully manoeuvred the lifeboat *Ann Ferguson* alongside and took off the crew of Russian Finns.

All Saints, the last remaining medieval church at Dunwich, was on the cliff above the beach. Every year more of the church fell over the cliff and the romantic story of 'the lost city under the sea' caught the imagination of Victorian authors, poets and artists. Dunwich became a tourist destination and some visitors believed the legend that the church bells could be heard from under the sea. Summer visitors also were taken out for trips in the Dunwich fishing boats and this provided summer work for the fishermen. The first Flora Tea Room built here had a name board from the barque *Flora* of Olland.

The Victorian visitors took little notice of the Dunwich beach village; a collection of wooden sheds, smoke houses, gear stores and public house 'The Ark' on the hill. All these slowly went into the sea and the last shed went in during three bad storms in the winter of 1911-12.

Apart from over the Dunwich Bank, the sea in front of Dunwich is a good deep-water fishing ground. In the 1950s the Dunwich boats were mainly fishing for herring that were sold to Lowestoft or people who came down on the beach. One man, George Lee, was lost while herring drifting. Local men searched the beach all night and eventually found the boat with his lighter and tobacco still on the thwart.

In the twentieth century there has been very little romance about 'Lost Dunwich'. The modern approach is totally different, and there has been a great curiosity about what actually lies under the sea. Stuart Bacon organised the first underwater survey of the 'lost city of Dunwich' in 1971. Dunwich fishermen were hired to take them out but the survey swiftly changed to using inflatable ribs, because of the difficulties in climbing over the high sides of the fishing boats.

A new era had began in 1963 when Phillip 'Dodger' Holmes and Rodney Collett, who had both worked on the construction of Sizewell Power Station, decided to have a joint venture fishing off Dunwich beach. When Phillip Holmes started, they landed 100 stone of fish a day regularly, but by 1994 this had dropped to an average of 20 stone a day.

Holmes and Collett's first boat was the *Hearts of Oak* and in about 1970 they had the *Two Sheilas* built and named her after their wives. In 1979 they had a new boat the 20.6ft x 8ft *Fred's Last* built by George 'Fred' Smeeth beside the River Stour at Dedham. Sadly Fred died before the boat was completed, and it had to be finished by another shipwright..

In 1972 Steve 'Pinger' King and his brother Mick King started commercial fishing at Dunwich in the *Brothers*. The demand for herring had gone, but they went drifting for sprat to bait their longlines for cod. They had long days in the boat as they used to go up to twelve miles off, anchor in 16-17 fathoms, shoot the lines for cod, wait for two hours and then haul them in.

By 1984 there were five boats full time and several part time boats fishing off Dunwich. In the winter a boat had two men to work the

Steve 'Pinger' King walking up to get his winch line to haul his beach boat *Jill Anne* ashore at Dunwich 2008.

In 2008 there were trials at Dunwich to try and save the beach. The 'Sausage' was an inexpensive type of groyne that local people liked because at least something was being done about the erosion. The 'sausages' here were covered by shingle quite quickly.

longlines, but in the summer they used to trawl single-handed. The average was 60 stone of cod in September, 30 stone in October and 15 stone in November. The best season for fishing was in May, when they went for 'spur dog' (dog fish) and sometimes landed 60-80 stone in a day.

In 1975 the Kings had the *Dingle Bight* built at Felixstowe Ferry. This new Dunwich boat was built with higher sides for this more exposed part of the coast. Another boat built by Andy Moore and John White at Felixstowe Ferry was the 20ft *Early & Late* with a 30hp Saab engine. 'Pinger' King had chosen this name because his brother Mick was often late and he had to go round to his house and give him a shout. 'Pinger' thought that a self-starter on an engine was more trouble than it was worth because they often got wet when coming ashore. He used to take the starters off and hand crank all his engines.

In 1991 Frank Knights (Shipwrights) built the last wooden boat for commercial fishing off a Suffolk beach at the Ferry Quay, Woodbridge. This was the 19ft 3ins x 9ft 5ins *Dodger* ordered by Phillip 'Dodger' Holmes at Dunwich. She was a very seaworthy boat and Marcus Gladwell told me he once met the *Dodger* some ten miles off shore, fishing in a gale.

The Dunwich Town Trust claims ownership of the beach and charge for each boat, winch and shed. Gales from the north or northwest cause a 'scouring tide' that damages the beach. The waves surge down the North Sea and erode the cliff foot. In October 1999 a severe overnight gale created a 4ft cliff in the shingle beach in front of the boats so that they could not be launched. This gale exposed the brick foundations of the old beach village that had eroded away in the Edwardian era.

Dunwich men believed that they lost about twelve weeks fishing a year, mostly in the winter, because the weather was too bad to get their boats off the beach. The method of getting afloat was to push the boat from the stern to get the bows into the sea as quickly as possible. If a powerful wave hit the bow it threw the boat sideways, and the next wave sent it back on the beach. In about 2000 Steve King adopted the new practice of having a wire and rope connected to an anchor laid at sea. The boat was launched off the beach bow first, with the power capstan on the boat pulling the anchor rope. All this was rigged up so that he could handle the boat single-handed.

The decline of fishing at Dunwich was caused by a series of factors starting with the dredging of sand from the seabed in front of Southwold. Cod fed on whelks that lived on the flint-covered seabed but as the dredging left a sandy bottom, without flints, there was less for the cod to feed on. The cod further reduced in the area when the green crab they lived on also vanished. Later the larger harbour boats started working the Dunwich waters with tangle nets. These are drift nets up to a mile long that drift along the bottom with the tide and catch everything.

Dunwich beach looked empty after Phillip Holmes sold the *Dodger* in 1998. For sixteen years after that Steve King fished alone in the summer with the strongly built 20ft *Jill Anne*, built at Felixstowe Ferry in about 1980, with a 30hp Saab engine. In 1994 Steve started reed cutting in the winter on the Dunwich and Walberswick level of marshes.

By 2000 Steve was catching more skate than in the past forty years, but as the authorities had no data on skate they wouldn't issue a quota. The last straw came when the seals starting eating fish out of the nets. As soon as Steve saw a seal's head pop out of the water, he started hauling his 30ft wide trawl, and at least managed to get what ever there was in the net at that time. The seals worked out what was going on and began diving under the water a long way off, before they were spotted, and then swam along the net and ate everything so that nothing was earned that day.

The golden years of fishing off beaches in Suffolk had been from about 1890-1914. The inter-war years saw a steady decline in boats, but the demand for food saw fishing pick up

Old well pumps, like this one on a boat at Walberswick, were used as bilge pumps on Southwold Harbour punts. In the sailing punts wooden scoops were used for bailing.

Punts at California, the southern end of Southwold beach, in about 1902.

after 1945 and from about 1970 there was another mini-golden age.

When a lorry collected the *Jill Anne* in 2013, and took her to Justine Ladd's yard at Southwold, no one seemed to notice that centuries of fishing from Dunwich had finally ended.

## Walberswick

*Dunwich Soul and Walberswick*
*All go in at lousy Cri'k (Creek)*
The people of the mid Suffolk coast have fought a heroic battle to stop erosion and keep the harbour mouth open so that Southwold could remain a port. In the medieval period Walberswick was an inland village up the Dunwich River, but erosion pushed the coast inland and Walberswick became a fishing village at the mouth of the river Blyth.

The sea beach in front of Walberswick was not used to land fishing boats, but there were capstans on the beach just above Walberswick Creek where inshore 'punts' were hauled up. On Southwold Harbour open boats were called punts because they were almost flat bottomed, but they were much the same design as other Suffolk beach boats. The village 'dock' was dug later on so that the Walberswick punts could be kept there. This was near the open foreshore known as The Flats where the cotton nets were hug out to dry to stop them rotting. The Flats used to help Walberswick support itself as an inshore fishing centre but this area is now used to collect revenue as a car park for tourists.

In about 1927 Billy English, who had a cottage next to 'The Bell,' spent sixteen weeks on a Lowestoft drifter and came home with the money to buy his first boat, the 18ft *Maud Ellen* for £8. This was complete with trawl and

Three generations of the Crittons building a small punt at Southwold in 1894. There were other builders in Southwold, but the Crittons appear to have tried new ideas.

shrimp trawl. In the late 1920s there was a major economic slump and many men looking for work went fishing off the beach in the hope of making a little money. One summer's day Billy English counted eighty-seven longshore fishing boats trawling off Southwold, mostly under sail, but a few were using old car engines.

In 2008 volunteers turned out to plant 3,000 Marram grass roots on the sandy beach in front of Walberswick. Marram grass holds the sand and prevents it from blowing off the beach and dunes are created. This form of sea defence has enjoyed some success on the Suffolk coast providing there is a long sloping beach to break the force of the waves.

## Southwold

A medieval sailor would not recognize the present coastline near Southwold, as it is totally different. In those days Eastern Bavents was the most easterly village in England and sat on a headland that has now totally vanished.

Just to the south the walled town of Dunwich sat on the next headland, while the Dunwich River was an estuary that snaked inland past Blythburgh. All the many trading and fishing vessels in the area must have operated from the Dunwich River. The fishermen only resorted to working off the beaches when erosion had taken away the best harbour on the coast.

In the age of sail, the coal trade was very important. Hundreds of small wooden sailing ships passed the East Anglian coast on their way from the North of England. On New Years Day in 1854 five hundred ships, which had been sheltering in Harwich Harbour arrived off Lowestoft and anchored waiting for a fair wind to the north. While they lay at anchor another five hundred ships arrived from the Thames and also anchored waiting for the weather to improve. Eventually a breeze from the southwest sprang up and some thousand sailing ships, anchored between Pakefield and The Cockle Gap, got 'under way' in one day. The sea was a mass of sails until they passed

Summer visitors flock around the punts to see what they have landed in about 1905.

After drifting, the normal practice was to return to the beach and shake the sprat out of the net on to a cloth. Three generations of the Palmer family are on Southwold beach with their punt, patriotically painted red, white and blue.

north over the horizon.

These colliers were often in a very poor state, and at the mercy of the weather, while their masters had very limited navigation aids. The only help they received was from the pilots and beach companies. Southwold was a good place for beach companies to operate. The beachmen manning the lookout towers on the high cliffs could see far out to sea, and the beach was a reasonably safe place to launch a yawl. As ships anchored regularly in Southwold Roads, just off the town, there was plenty of work putting pilots on ships and retrieving lost anchors.

A tombstone in Southwold churchyard, dated 1786, has a three masted, clinker lugger carved on it. This was the type of boat that had been used for fishing and pilotage. These luggers developed from the medieval three masters with square sails. The mariners found that if the yards on the sails were tilted they could sail closer to wind. But even in the eighteenth century, when the lug rig was widely used, they often turned the fore lug into a square sail when running down wind. The next development was for the central main mast to be 'left ashore'

but even when the luggers became two masted, they still called the taller mast the foremast.

The Southwold pilots were a rough old crowd, both ashore and afloat. At the beginning of the nineteenth century a custom had grown up that the first yawl to reach a vessel for pilotage or salvage got the work. The Southwold pilots were determined to be the first to board a ship and this developed into open warfare. In 1814 the yawl *Jubilee* sank a rival yawl and in 1855 the *Swiftsure* rammed the *Reliance*. Three years later the *Cricketer* turned the *Trazer* over and in another incident a man was killed in a fight outside the Long Island Watch House.

Pilotage was a major business and the beach companies had fast lightweight yawls to get pilots aboard in coastal waters. In the early Victorian period there were also five decked pilot cutters working out of the harbour. Southwold cutters such as the *Cynthia* and *Prudence* are reputed to have cruised almost as far as Norway in search of a ship needing a pilot to London or any East Coast port.

The centre of the Southwold beach fishing community was the 'beach village' at the bottom of the cliff in front of the town where a few people had small cottages. Most of the beach village was a collection of black-tarred clapboard sheds, with tiled roofs. These sheds were used as fishermen's gear stores, smoke houses and for net tanning. Boats were hauled up using the hand capstans, known in Southwold as 'bulls' because of the power they developed.

Between 1846-70 James Critten is reputed to have built six beach yawls and numerous other boats in a shed in the beach village, but when the sheds were swept away the Crittens moved up into the town. Every storm nibbled away at the beach village. In one storm Ben Herrington fled for his life and lost everything when the sea swept away his house, boats and even two pigsties.

A young woman called Charlotte Ellis asked the vicar of Southwold why the fishermen didn't come to church. The Vicar replied; 'You had better go and ask them that' so Charlotte did. The fishermen said they had to go to sea when the fish were there. Charlotte was not going to be beaten and decided that if the fishermen wouldn't come to church she would start Sunday evening Bible Readings in the old Lifeboat Shed. This proved to be very popular and men, women and children flocked to the Readings.

Some local worthies protested to the Bishop that a woman was preaching on the beach, but she managed to convince the Bishop that she was just reading the Bible. However her mission ended abruptly in 1862 when a storm washed the Old Lifeboat Shed away. Another lady, Francis Rayley, saved the day by having the Sailor's Reading Room built, on the cliff top, in 1864. No alcohol was allowed in this Reading Room as it was primarily intended to keep the

The beach below Kilcock Hill in around 1895. In the centre is one of the carrying 'bullock' yawls and on the left the two men are holding a draws'l that was used on the Suffolk coast, on calm days, by being lowered over the bow so that the tide pulled the boat along.

Southwold fishermen in leather boots baiting longlines.

men out of the public houses.

The beachmen of Southwold seem to have been only loosely organized into companies that kept changing their names. North America had captured the imaginations of the Southwold longshoremen because early settlers had gone to Long Island from Southwold. In 1810 the Long Island beach company was formed and had its Watch House built in 1841 on the highest point of the cliff, in front of the present Reading Room. This Watch House was eventually washed away in a severe storm in March 1906. The New York Company's Watch House was at the southern end of the cliff but due to erosion this was demolished in 1853. The sandy beach near the harbour was known as California and another company began working from here at one stage. The Gun Hill became known as the New York cliff and by 2014 the beach huts here were the most expensive in Southwold. These were changing hands for £100,000 even though ground rent still had to be paid.

In 1829 the Kilcock Company built a Watch House and later had a shed beside the path down to the beach village in front of the town. In 1890 this company had a third yawl called *Bittern* built. This yawl was fitted out to be rowed with eight oars each side. Although the main pilotage work had gone, she became the pride of Southwold at the beach regattas.

The *Bittern* was mostly crewed by the Smith family and once when she returned from Kessingland Regatta someone asked coxswain 'Winner' Smith the names of the other yawls that had been there. He replied; 'I don't know, I only saw them at the start.' The *Bittern's* great rival was the Lowestoft yawl *Georgiana* and these two were the only yawls in the last race in 1910, when the *Bittern* won.

The arrival of the railway brought more summer visitors to Southwold. The shopkeepers and hoteliers saw this as a new opportunity for the town to develop tourism and the fishermen were slowly pushed off the central beach. Some fishermen used to operate the bathing machines used by summer visitors.

The last company operating at Southwold was the Kilcock Company that had been forced to move to the north of the pier and was then sometimes known as the North Company. In the 1920s the Kilcock Company was still using its carrying yawls *John Bull* and *Baden Powell* to recover anchors. By then the Beach Company members had become too elderly and the famous yawl *Bittern* was presented to the town, to be a memorial to generations of beachmen.

Southwold Harbour, 1970. Joe Palmer is mending a beam trawl in his punt *Arthur & Phyllis*.

The Suffolk beach boat *LT 792* oil on linen by James Dodds. The Southwold punt's yellow cove line always looked smart.

The 48ft *Bittern* being sailed off the North Beach, Southwold. The mizzen is almost set and the men forward are getting the foresail up to drag her off the beach.

The yawl *Bittern* sailing off Southwold Pier. The Southwold fishermen usually wore white smocks while the Lowestoft men favoured brown smocks.

Roger Finch's drawing of the 40ft yawl *Baden* Powell that had been abandoned on Southwold beach in 1930.

ROGER FINCH.

The Southwold fishermen's sheds were moved off the beach in wartime so that troops would have clear line of fire if there were an invasion.

Sadly she was left out in the open and her hull rotted away. A superb model of this famous yawl can be seen in the Sailor's Reading Room and her rudder is still outside.

The yawls were the stars of old time beach regattas, held all along the coast, but the punts raced as well. One of the crack racing skippers was Billy 'Barr' Stannard who sailed in the *Smiling Morn*, built by Critten in 1903. She was sloop rigged to run trips off the beach in the summer, but was given a lug rig to race with the punts. Barr Stannard used a leeboard on the *Smiling Morn*; basically a plank put down over the side. Some of the gear from *Smiling Morn* finished up over the bar of 'The Bell' at Walberswick. This included the leeboard and oars that had old horse harness wrapped around them to prevent chafing.

After he had won the coveted Elms Cup at Southwold, Stannard became nicknamed 'Barr' after the famous America Cup skipper Barr. His son 'Ernie' Stannard remembered that they once left Southwold harbour to sail to Aldeburgh Regatta when the seas were 'steeple

deep.' Next day they raced around a triangular course and Barr gained time by swinging the lug around in front of the mast, instead of dipping it around aft. This manoeuvre was only possible in a light breeze. When the wind freshened most of the boats were reefed, but Barr carried on with a full foresail and won.

In about 1910 about forty-eight boats were kept on Southwold beach. Many men worked on the boats part time and at other times worked in the building trade, cutting reeds and anything else that came along. In the autumn they returned to drift net fishing for sprat with two or three men aboard each boat. Many families survived by buying 'on tick' in Southwold shops. At the beginning of the sprat season the men bought new leather boots, but if the sprat fishery failed the shops risked going broke.

In 1905 Southwold residents had a wake up call when a dramatic storm and high tide swept away the last of the beach village. Better groynes were constructed along the beach and steps were built down the crumbling cliff so that

Southwold beach being 'recharged' with sand dredged out in the North Sea, 2006.

life could carry on as normal. In the 1930s more groynes were put in place and a concrete wall and walkway, were built along the sea front. However in 1938 a northerly gale damaged the pier and smashed some of the beach huts on the sea front.

In May 1964 we had a day out with friends who had hired a beach hut at Southwold. Although the children enjoyed being on the beach I found it boring and went up the cliff steps and discovered the Sailor's Reading Room.

The Reading Room walls were covered with faded photographs, a true record of Southwold when it was a beach fishing 'station.' The model of the open lugger *Rapid* shows that she must have been one of the finest 'punts' built. Seated around a scrubbed topped table, wearing their peaked caps and blue ganseys, were a group of retired fishermen. I sat down and started talking to them and steered the conversation back into the age of sail. I was told of the day when about sixty Southwold punts were at sea when a sudden NE gale swept down the coast. Most of these were the open 18ft punts, which would not have

survived the breakers crashing ashore.

The fleet took the time honoured course of the sailors caught at sea and ran before the wind, in this case south, round Orfordness. Here they close hauled their sails and managed to get into Orford Haven, at the mouth of the River Ore. The fleet then made its way up to Orford and a telegram was sent back to Southwold to say that they were all safe. The boats were hauled ashore and sails put over them to make tents to live in. Fish were sold to get a little money to buy food and when the weather calmed down they returned to Southwold.

A great admirer of the Southwold beachmen was Ernest Read Cooper, a solicitor and the Town Clerk of Southwold, who had been born at Blythburgh Lodge in 1865. Ernest Cooper was the first person to record seriously the activities of the Suffolk beachmen and wrote books including the 'Storm Warriors.' Cooper believed that the prosperity of Southwold depended on it having a good harbour. Good harbours cost money, but he raised the capital to renew the piers on either

The 44ft Norfolk and Suffolk lifeboat *Alfred Corry* being launched into a whole gale from the South Beach, Southwold, 1896. The crew are hauling on the rope laid out to an anchor while the men ashore are pushing her out with 'setts,' long poles. The *Alfred Corry* was launched forty-one times and saved forty-seven lives between 1893-1918.

side of the harbour mouth and provided a new harbour quay and fish market. In 1907 the first herrings were landed from the North Sea fishery, mostly by Scottish boats from the Moray Firth. Sadly, because Southwold harbour was too far south and fishermen needed extra sailing time to get there, the 1912 season was the last time the Scottish boats came.

In the Victorian period beachmen switched over from undertaking rescues in beach yawls to using the RNLI lifeboats, but they demanded to have lifeboats that could be sailed. This led to a class of lifeboat known as the Norfolk and Suffolk that had smaller sails than the yawls, but was more substantially built.

In 1893 the new Norfolk and Suffolk 44ft lifeboat *Alfred Corry* arrived at Southwold from Lowestoft with fisherman John Cragie as coxswain. She was kept in a shed near the harbour pier and when launched into the sea the crew hauled on a warp to an offshore anchor while men on the shore pushed her with 'setting' poles. This lifeboat had a crew of seventeen men

and required the help of most of Southwold fishermen to get her afloat. The very last Norfolk and Suffolk lifeboat in service was withdrawn in 1947 but long before that the *Alfred Corry* had become a yacht.

In 1977 John Cragie, a Trinity House Pilot and great-grandson of the original coxswain, found the *Alfred Corry* as a derelict houseboat at Maldon. He fitted her out to sail as a yacht and eventually brought her back to Southwold where a splendid group of volunteers have restored her back to the appearance as a Victorian sailing lifeboat.

During World War I the beach was closed and the capstans and boats were moved into Southwold Harbour. After the war Joe Palmer used his gratuity money to build the *Arthur & Phyllis*, in 1919. This was the last sailing punt built but Joe intended to fit an engine as soon as he earned enough money. When boats were fitted with engines they had enough power to push them over the tide in and out of the harbour. To begin with fishermen used to pull their boats up on to the harbour beach, but gradually jetties

Volunteers have restored the sailing and pulling lifeboat, *Alfred Corry*. She is housed in the former 1923 Cromer Lifeboat Shed that was brought to Southwold in 1998.

were constructed.

In 1938 King George VI visited the popular youth summer camp at Southwold and arrived in the Royal Yacht *Victoria & Albert (III)*. The King was brought in shore by a launch and then rowed ashore in a punt by the fishermen Prim Deal and Dykes Stannard.

In World War II a 'block' ship was sunk across the harbour mouth and the entrance silted up with sand. Southwold beach was mined and scaffold pole barriers put up to prevent the enemy from landing. After the war five boats were worked from the beach. The Jarvis' had a boat just north of the pier while Vic Boggis worked his small punt *Billy* from the foot of Eastern Bavents cliff.

In 1948 'Dusso' Winter wanted a fishing boat and bought the old Critten-built 16ft punt *Faith* that was on the beach. She was too small to have an engine and the old men used to say that her hull was so ancient that an engine would have shaken her to bits. 'Dusso's' seventeen year old son John 'Dusso' Winter, later a fisherman and sometimes mayor of Southwold, remembered that they 'worked the tides' and when fishing under sail it was often quicker to row up wind rather than tack. Fishermen kept to the lug rig because it was a 'lifting sail' that could be lowered and stowed out of the way when working the fishing gear. The alternative was the gaff rig, which is a 'pressing sail' and needs plenty of stays to take the strain off the mast and the boom was always in the way. The only time the gaff rig was used at Southwold and Aldeburgh was for running pleasure trips in the summer. With passengers aboard a dipping lugsail would have been impossible to work.

By 1981 there were just a few rotten hulls lying amongst the beach huts in front of the town. Southwold Harbour remained a successful fishing port and eight commercial fishing boats remained in 2014. The harbour was also the home of *Dodger, Arthur & Phyllis, Valsand* and several other wooden punts.

An early attempt at Kessingland to hold back the sea was made by using hazel faggots. However the Beach End was still being threatened in the 1930s.

In 1936 there was a serious attempt at creating sea defences at Kessingland.

In 1936 a portable narrow gauge railway was used at Kessingland to bring in material for sea defences and this appears to have held the line until better defences were built. In 1953 a concrete wall was being built when the Floods occurred.

## Benacre Ness

As Covehithe Ness eroded away the land to the north became Benacre Ness. On the 1910 map there is a boathouse near the Hundred River entrance and 'lifeboats' are marked at the end of a road going down to a beach. Even during World War II the Ness was a headland in front of Tim Crick's Beach Farm. Here the soil appears to have moved north to fill up the beach in front of Kessingland. In World War II a road was built down here so that shingle could be carted away to build vital airfield runaways. There used to be three shingle pits here and two have already gone under the sea.

The St Jude Day tide of December 2013 took four metres of land off Benacre Ness in front of Beach Farm. After this the Environmental Agency brought in 370 tonne of rock to protect the foreshore and stop the Hundred River Pumping Station from being washed away. Benacre Estate manager, Edward Vere Nicoll,

said that the estate was loosing 20 acres a year into the sea, a considerable area of land for a small island nation to lose.

## Kessingland

### Beach End

In the medieval period ships used Kessingland Haven, but in the early fourteenth century the sand bar closed the Haven mouth. With their harbour gone the men had little option but to work fishing boats off the open beach.

The old beachmen called Kessingland 'Kess'el,' and the settlement near the landing was known as the Beach End. The main income from fishing was from the autumn drift netting for herring and sprat. As the sea was shallow around Benacre Ness the fishermen couldn't trawl in the summer, so they used nets to take salmon near the Ness.

The Kessingland Beach Company had a lookout on the low cliff and was the last

Landing sprat at Kessingland about 1937. The boats were often loaded down to their top planks and then rowed ashore, but this boat still has her foresail set. The sail is tightly made fast to either end of the yard, but longshore lugger sailors believed that the sail was more effective if it was 'four fingers' away from the yard in the centre. The sprat nets are being shaken out on to an old sail and the net being loaded on to a barrow ready to go back in the boat.

it was withdrawn in 1936, but they kept their shed as a social meeting place.

In those days the fishermen who manned the East Anglian lifeboats expected to share in any salvage money raised by a rescue. Arthur Hunt, with whom I first went to sea in the early 1950s, had a deep hatred of lifeboats and whenever we saw one he used to grumble. 'There they are, salvage sharks robbing the poor sailormen.' I think this was an attitude left over from the days when Arthur was young and he was going north in a boomie barge to get coal and the beach yawls were still hovering around like vultures looking for ships in trouble.

When 'Cock Robin' Brown started fishing in 1921 there were twenty-eight boats fishing from Kessingland. In the drift net season each boat had a crew of three men so that there were about sixty men getting a living fishing off this beach. While ashore, the older men used to help get the boats up the beach and others helped with net mending and boat building.

In the early nineteenth century the Suffolk men abandoned the old pointed 'double ended' boats and went over to shallow draft beamy boats with transom sterns. These seem to have worked well on the shingle beaches, which were often steep, while further north beaches were shallow. For this reason the Norfolk fishermen kept their double-ended boats because the pointed sterns parted the steep waves astern when they were coming ashore. In Norfolk the last wooden double-ended boat built for crabbing was the 22ft *Valerie*

company in Suffolk to operate. In 1906 the Kessingland Company had forty members, all oldish men. However the steam drifter owner Arthur Gouldby gave the Company a new shed and this brought it back to life. Well wishers gave the company a new yawl, the *Sophia (III)* in 1912, but she was only launched a few times, and was once sailed to Southwold. Sadly she was left to rot on the beach. When the cliff started to slide down, the Company shed was moved a little to the south on the flat ground at the bottom of the road. The beach company men took over running the RNLI lifeboat until

The last beach boats race was held, at Kessingland, in 1948.

*Teresa* in 1989 and many fibreglass traditional double-enders were built after that.

However in Suffolk some men at Southwold and Kessingland kept their pointed stern boats. In about 1985 Roy Brown told me that there had been four double-ended boats at Kessingland and one of these, the *Gladys,* usually won the beach

The Kessingland Boat Shed, in 1986, with 'Cock Robin' Brown standing outside. The telescope hole in the shed was used to check that boats were safe at sea. The shed still had faded Victorian photographs and ships portraits on the walls and old fishermen used to gather here for a yarn.

regattas. In these races Brown's 18ft *Bessie* often finished in the first three.

The herring usually came inshore at the end of September and there was anxiety if they didn't turn up. Once, when the herring shoals had not arrived the Browns set out in the *Bessie,* early one morning, to sail out towards the Smith's Knoll where they had heard that there were plenty of herring. They knew that several of the steam drifters, owned and manned by men from Kessingland, would be heading back to the Lowestoft fish market. The men on the Kessingland drifter they met had all been beachmen at some stage and were happy to give their mates some fish. They willingly filled up the 'fish rooms' between the two forward thwarts on the *Bessie.*

The Browns then sailed the *Bessie* to Lowestoft, where the herring were sold in the fish market and they then rowed round to the coal dock and collected coal for ballast. After this they sailed back to Kessingland beach with coal for

The beach boat LT278 seen here in 2006. She was the last of the Kessingland fishing boats on the beach but was burnt not long after this.

household fires.

In about 1967 Roy Brown and his son were coming ashore in bad weather in the *Bessie* when the hauling up wire broke and she was swamped and sank. The Browns got ashore, but the boat remained there for a tide with breakers crashing over her. Sadly the boat was badly damaged and was hauled ashore to end her days rotting away behind the sheds.

The 18.5ft x 7.9ft x 1.8ft Kessingland boat *Valsand*, named after the owner's two daughters, is the only Suffolk beach boat to have briefly achieved a national profile. In 1955 the BBC radio programme 'Down to the Sea' featured the *Valsand* making a voyage from Southwold to Burnham Overy. The *Valsand* had been built at North Beach, Lowestoft by Frank Fuller in 1948 as a motorboat, but her owner 'Hurricane' Brown found a foresail and mizzen and half the trip was made under sail. The mate on this BBC expedition was 'Hurricane's' 72-year-old uncle, Alfred Brown.

After leaving Southwold the *Valsand's* first overnight stop was to go ashore at Kessingland.

Here they went into the fisherman's boat shed in the evening and heard tales of the old beach regattas held before World War I when the rival beach yawls, the 48ft *Bittern* from Southwold and 48ft *Georgiana* from Lowestoft, battled it out to win.

Next morning, following the age-old tradition, the crew of the *Westward* helped to get the *Valsand* into the water and in return they helped *Westward* to be launched. Continuing on their passage north the *Valsand's* crew commented how few boats were out longshore fishing when in fine weather. Forty years before, the whole coastal sea would have been dotted with inshore fishing boats.

In 1936 'Cock Robin' Brown had the 18.6ft *Result* built at Kessingland and this was the last longshore boat built here. She had a full set of lugsails, but was fitted with an engine and had a central prop shaft under the stern. In 1981 the *Result* was one of only four boats kept on a tiny strip of shingle right up against the concrete walkway. When 'Cock Robin' Brown was in his eighties he still went out fishing, even though he had to be helped over the side of the boat.

In the 1930s the houses at Beach End were very nearly lost under the waves but fortunately the sea defences at Kessingland held. Even after the concrete wall was built, just after World War II, it had been touch and go for a long time. Then shingle and sand began to build up and the distance from the concrete wall to the beach gradually increased as a marram grass wilderness formed. However in the autumn of 2013 four angling boats were kept on the edge of the Denes with waves breaking on the beach in front of them. No fishing boats were kept on Kessingland beach after the December 5 surge tide swept along the coast.

## Gisleham

It is assumed that in the medieval period, ships with cargoes for Gisleham used to go up the Kessingland Haven to a quay in the Black Street area. After the haven closed the ships were discharged on the open beach, somewhere near the old lighthouse site, until the nineteenth century.

## Pakefield

*The Roaring Boys of Pakefield*
*Oh Lord how they do thrive*
*They had but one poor Parson*
*And they buried him alive.*

It seems that one evening in about 1800 the Pakefield parson decided to take a walk on the beach. At the same time the Pakefield smugglers were making a 'run' ashore with a load of contraband. Since they could not buy or frighten the parson into silence they buried him up to his armpits in the beach and when their night's work was done, sent someone from the village to released the unfortunate man.

The beach at Pakefield faces the sheltered anchorage of Lowestoft South Roads. About a mile and a half off the beach is the Newcombe Sand that creates some shelter from the worst of the North Sea weather.

When the Church of St Margaret and All

Boats on Pakefield beach covered up for the winter with the church of St Margaret and All Saints in the background.

Pakefield beach with Lowestoft Harbour in the background, 2013.

Saints at Pakefield was built, it stood in open countryside about a mile inland. In 1800 the church was still half a mile away from the sea, but in 1930 the beach was only 10m from church wall. Since 1800 erosion by the sea has taken about 200 acres of land and 120 houses, a considerable loss. Not only a loss of valuable land, but more countryside inland was taken up for building new houses. The loss of homes was very dramatic: often several houses went in one storm, but in the 1930s the authorities finally reacted and started to put groynes in to hold the beach in place. The erosion was stopped in 1945 when a concrete sea wall and more groynes were constructed on the beach. This helped to create the marram grass wilderness that stretches north from Benacre Ness.

In 1860 there were classes for 18ft and 16ft 'lug sailed' inshore fishermen's boats at the Pakefield and Kirkley Regatta. In the 1880s Pakefield was the home for seventy beachmen who operated their beach company. They raced the yawl *Sir Savill Crossley* and there was also a lifeboat here. Most of old fishing village went

under the sea and the streets that once led down to the nineteenth century beach landing now ends abruptly on the cliff.

Since 1934 Pakefield has been part of Lowestoft. The old photographs of Pakefield beach in the 1930s only show a couple of pleasure boats there and when George Chapman moved here in 1943 there were no full time fishermen. George went rod and line fishing in the 1950s and said that there were plenty of fish; he used to go just 300 yards out to get cod and the herring that came close inshore.

In 2013 about twenty-four boats were kept on the beach for angling and herring drifting in the autumn, mostly operating inside the Newcombe and Barnard Banks. Sometimes Pakefield boats had to go out sixteen miles to find enough fish.

Most boat owners on the beach shared motor winches, but there was a splendid collection of veteran motor winches rusting away. Almost unbelievably, two of the old wooden capstans from the sailing beach boat days were still there.

On December 5, 2013 George's daughter phoned him to tell him that the big tide was

In 2014 Pakefield beach had an oak hand capstan and several of the old iron motor winches that had survived the St Judes day surge tide.

forecast for 10.30pm, but the sea had already come up much higher than normal. The sea was crashing over the beach rising up to the foot of the cliff and a group of men were on the beach pulling the boats back. George's boat, one of only two wooden boats on the beach, had to be hauled back from hanging over a small shingle cliff that had formed on the edge of the beach. That night the tide took 16ft of shingle off the seaward side of the beach.

This was the highest tide since 1953, but no one was drowned and damage to property was only a fraction of what it had been sixty years before. It justified all the sea and river defences made along the East Coast since the disastrous 1953 Floods.

In 2014 there were nine registered fishermen at Pakefield, mostly retired men with fishing in their blood. They were usually drift netting for herring and pilchard and selling their catch from their houses. The 'Roaring Boys' have long gone from Pakefield beach; they have been replaced by more peaceful folk taking their dogs for a walk along the coastal path.

# Lowestoft

*Beachman's children's prayer*

*God bless Mum and Dad*
*And send us a wreck before daylight*

### North and South Beach

For centuries Lowestoft, or Loes'toff to the locals, was a port without a harbour and everything had to be landed on the open beach. There had been an estuary here, but coastal erosion had blocked the entrance with a wide belt of sand denes. Since there was a thriving North Sea herring fishery there was plenty of work for the beachmen ferrying fish ashore. When writing in 1790 Gillingwater recorded that two hundred and fifty years before, in the time of Henry VIII, there had been three fathoms (five and half metres) of water in front of the town but this area had become dry land. There used to be a huge area of denes that were flooded on surge tides and were constantly eroding and moving. The remains of the sunken denes

The 40ft 14 oared Lowestoft lifeboat *Frances Ann* is regarded as being the first sailing lifeboat and a prototype of the Norfolk and Suffolk lifeboat class. Here, in 1820, she was going to assist a ship on the Holm Sand. The horses are no doubt waiting to pull her back up the beach.

A proud horse owner in about 1880, near a beach yawl.

became offshore sandbanks and after the Battle of Waterloo an effigy of Napoleon was put up on these sands. In 1861 the Holm Sand was still dry enough for beachmen to take people out there on trips.

Because Lowestoft was a good landing place the North Sea herring were brought ashore and auctioned off on the beach. In calm weather the luggers were run ashore, but in bad weather the beachmen had to ferry in their catch. The fishery steadily expanded so that there was a need for more labour in the beach area. Gillingwater recorded that the first houses were built on the denes in 1790 and this grew into the Beach Village, quite separate from the old town on the cliff top. The Beach or 'the Grit' was linked to old Lowestoft by twelve narrow alleys known as Scores. A century later the Beach Village had expanded so that as well as the clapboard-clad beachmen sheds and smokehouses for smoking fish there were thirteen public houses and over a thousand people living here. This was considerably larger than any of the other beach settlements that had grown up along the Suffolk coast in the nineteenth century.

At Lowestoft the first mention of beachmen having clubbed together to operate yawls was in 1762. The work must have increased because in the 1780s three more companies had started. By the end of the eighteenth century the Lowestoft companies were well organised. Joseph Denny's Company had a gear store and lookout tower near the Ness and seems to have been putting pilots aboard ships down the Suffolk coast as far as Hollesley Bay.

Putting pilots on to passing ships was the Company's bread and butter work while salvage was the icing on the cake. Some pilots were licensed to take ships across the North Sea to Elsinore, Denmark, on their way to the Baltic to collect timber. In bad weather fleets of ships regularly anchored under the shelter of the sandbanks in Lowestoft Roads. Many ships lost their anchors and in fine weather the beachmen used their heavy yawls to drag grapples along the seabed and 'swipe' for lost anchors. In the next gale these were taken out and sold to vessels in trouble.

Lowestoft changed dramatically in 1831 when a channel was cut through the denes. The increased the fishing and trade into the new harbour changed Lowestoft into a very busy Victorian industrial town.

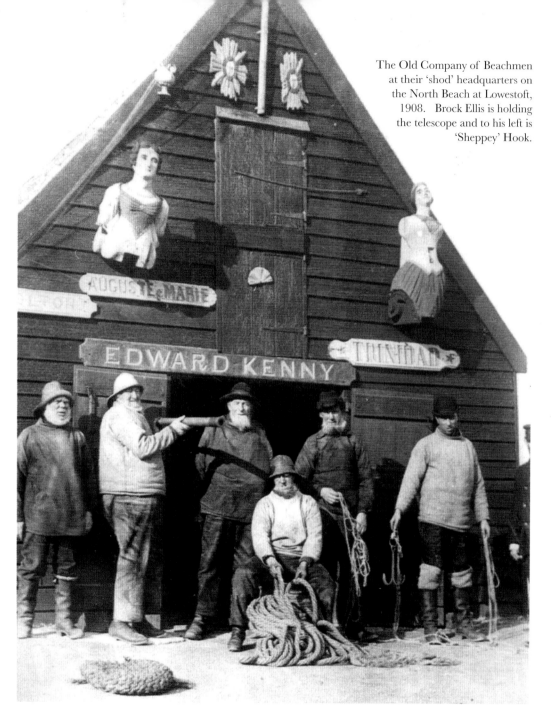

The Old Company of Beachmen at their 'shod' headquarters on the North Beach at Lowestoft, 1908. Brock Ellis is holding the telescope and to his left is 'Sheppey' Hook.

The opening of the harbour robbed the beachmen of their age-old work of ferrying fish ashore. It also meant that the pilots could then operate cutters from the harbour. It appears that the pilots had owned and controlled the yawls, but three years after the harbour opened everything had changed. The pilots left and the true salvage companies were formed with the beachmen being shareholders in the ownership of the companies and the yawls. The advantage of continuing to work off the beach was that boats with sail and oar could get to sea quickly when similar craft could have had trouble getting out of the dangerous harbour entrance.

The pride of the Old Company was the 50ft yawl *Happy New Year* (V). Here, she is leaving Lowestoft Harbour with a racing crew, in about 1900.

Various forms of beach companies were found from Mundesley right round to Felixstowe Ferry. David Huggins listed 208 beach yawls built in Norfolk and Suffolk. The beach companies also owned many gigs, galleys and small boats. But there was nothing to equal the East Anglian beach yawls; they were the fastest sailing workboats in the British Isles.

The beach companies were run from the public houses where the men used to draw their wages or 'doles.' Joseph Denny of the 'Herring Fishery' organised a beach company as did William Lincoln of the 'Jolly Maltsters.' In the 1835 reorganisation Denny's became known as the Old Company while Read's, Lincoln's and Cox's became the Young Company. A little later a breakaway group of beachmen formed the North Roads Company and operated from the 'George and Dragon.'

The pride of each company was their yawls, always called 'yolls' by the longshoremen. The term 'yoll' probably came from the Danish 'jolle,' meaning an open clinker boat, and the open boats of the East Anglian coast remained very similar to their Scandinavian origins.

At the beginning of the nineteenth century the yawls were beamy and seaworthy, but the competition between the beach companies to reach a vessel first was fierce and light, narrow, fast yawls where created. The 68ft three-masted yawl *Reindeer*, built in 1838, carried eighty-five people and is credited with sailing on a broad reach at 16 knots. The yawl *Mosquito*, built at Lowestoft in 1853 for the Young Company, was the first yawl with two masts. In effect the mainmast had been removed but beachmen continued to call their largest sail the foresail.

The whole Beach Village came alive when there was a cry of 'Running Down!' Getting these sizeable craft into water quickly required co-operation of whole community. Everyone ran to help launch a yawl as they were then entitled to have a share of the salvage money. Sometimes men ran into the water and touched the yawl to claim a share.

Once the skids were placed under the bow,

The Young Company's 48.6ft x 9ft x 6ft *Georgiana* is flying her racing prize flags on the North Beach, Lowestoft. Jack Swan was at the tiller. He was regarded as being the best 'timoneer,' (helmsman) who sailed an East Anglian yawl.

ballast to keep her upright. Sailing these yawls was a highly skilled business that needed a large crew. When the yawl returned a crowd used to gather on the beach to hear of their exploits. In 1982 I spoke to a retired shipwright who said he could remember the *Georgiana* on the Lowestoft North Beach. She had been hauled up on a chain, by a horse walking around a 'crab capstan.'

The mid-Victorian era was the golden era of the beach companies and every gale blew them more salvage work. In the 1880s three hundred beachmen were members of the three Lowestoft beach companies but the steam tugs and the RNLI lifeboats steadily took away their role. When the tugs first started towing vessels off the sands the beachmen were very angry and pelted them with stones from their ballast bags. The beach companies were powerful local institutions and took over the running of the RNLI lifeboats. In 1882, to be independent of the RNLI and their beachmen crews, the private lifeboat *Caroline Hamilton* was built and based at Lowestoft.

there was a shout of 'Hold her up!' and the bilge stools were pulled away allowing the yawl to be 'run' down the beach. The sacks of shingle ballast were only put in when the yawls were afloat. The crews then rushed through the water and scrambled aboard. Out came the oars and they fought to get her through the breaking waves as the great foresail was set. When the wind filled the sail the yawl shot away. As they gathered speed the pressure on the hull made the planks creak, while spray was thrown away from the bow and six men had to bail furiously to throw the water over the leeward side. Other members of the crew trimmed the

Yawls racing at Lowestoft.

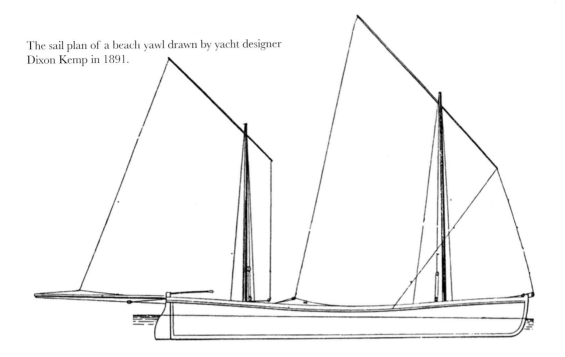

The sail plan of a beach yawl drawn by yacht designer Dixon Kemp in 1891.

The beach regattas for workboats were well established in the 1850s and these fuelled the rivalry between the beach companies. The towns supported the regattas because they provided a spectacle for the summer visitors to watch. The sight of the great luggers cutting through the sea thrilled the visitors.

Although beach company work was declining, thirteen yawls took part in a race in 1887 and the following year sixteen yawls raced, crewed by four hundred beachmen. The 1888 race was won by the Young Company's yawl *Success* with Jack Swan at the tiller. In 1892

the Young Company's yawl *Young Prince* was considered to be unfit to race and admirers, mostly shopkeepers and wealthy men, raised the money for the 48ft *Georgiana* to be built by Allerton. She was designed by Capps, a member of a Lowestoft fishing family and was sailed by Jack Swan. The day after she was launched the *Georgiana* beat the Southwold *Bittern* and yawls from the Norfolk beaches. After this she went on to win fifteen yawl races.

Not to be beaten, the Old Company commissioned George Watson, a leading yacht designer of the day, to design a faster yawl. This

The Lowestoft tripper yawl *Amity*, stripped out ready for a rebuild, at Brancaster.

Will Buckenham's 1760 Old Smokehouse in Raglan Street, Lowestoft.

became harbour based; they remained clinker and open but often had a little cuddy forward and sometimes a jib was set.

The beachmen's main work changed in the summer to running summer trips for the 'holiday makers.' This called for a new type of 'yoll;' smaller, beamy, double ended and rigged as a gaff sloop. Some worked from the South Beach in Kirkley and were owned by David Cook and others. The only surviving Suffolk pleasure yoll is the 37ft *Amity*, built in 1912 for the Butcher Brothers to run trips off the beach. During World War I the German Navy shelled Lowestoft for twenty minutes in April 1916 and one shell blew a wooden pile through *Amity's* bow. After this the Brancaster mussel fisherman Loose bought her and had the bow repaired. She worked in North Norfolk until 1960 when she became a yacht. In 2014 the Loose family put the *Amity* into a shed intending to restore her.

In Lowestoft's heyday as a 'herring town' there were dozens of smokehouses curing fish; many were small sheds in people's back gardens. By 2014 there were only three commercial smokehouses working in the town. These were the Raglan Street smokehouse, the Anchor on Katwiyk Way and the J & K Smokery, in the Beach Industrial Area near the fish market. This smokehouse, formerly Butcher's, run by James Brown and his son was the most easterly surviving building from the old Beach Village. It is a small brick building with a tiled roof and a modern building on the side. The walls inside the old brick smokehouse are thick with black

was the 50ft *Happy New Year* launched in 1894 and although she never equalled the *Georgiana* she did win the final Lowestoft yawl race in 1907.

In 1897 a surge tide swept over Lowestoft beach and some beachmen returned from sea to find their homes had been flooded. The newspapers at the time reported this was the ninth major flood in the nineteenth century. Flooding caused terrible suffering to people and was expensive to businesses. The Victorian and Edwardian eras were ages of great confidence. Britain had created the world's largest empire, so that dealing with the North Sea was not seen as a great problem. To protect the Beach Village the Douglas Wall was built in 1902-03 and was the first seawall with groynes on the North Beach. This sea wall was very successful for the next thirty years but it had made it difficult to launch boats. As a result the Lowestoft inshore fishing boats

Jim Brown in his smokehouse in the Beach Industrial Area, Lowestoft, 2014. To smoke the fish they are hung up across the room above four oak fires on the floor. The fish in cages are filleted kippers.

tar from decades of smoking. In 2015 four oak fires on the floor were cold smoking fish. This process only preserves the fish and they have to be cooked, but hot smoked, ready to eat, mackerel, salmon and hake were smoked in the modern building next door.

Suffolk boat builders used to be trained in the boatyards along the coast, but from 1975 the International Boatbuilding Training College in Lowestoft was opened to train shipwrights to work in wooden boat construction. In 2014, when run by Gill and Nat Wilson, a Suffolk beach boat was built on the lines of the Aldeburgh boat *Ossie*. This was the first new wooden beach boat built in Suffolk since the *Dodger* in 1991.

In the interwar years the Science Museum in London realised that all the traditional sailing workboats of Britain were just about to die out. They employed Naval Architects to go round and measure the lines of boats around the whole coast. William Blake was paid to go and measure the East Coast

boats and found the 15.2ftx 6.3ftx 2.4ft *Ossie* on Aldeburgh beach. Built by Critten at Southwold in 1893 this boat had sunk off Aldeburgh and the three men aboard had been rescued.

## Corton

The Romans had a Signal Station at Corton on high ground south of the mouth of Yarmouth Haven. In 1337 Corton was further inland overlooking the mouth of Yarmouth Haven. The spit of land on the seaward side eroded away and the Haven entrance moved north about five miles to the present entrance at Gorleston.

Before the harbour entrance was cut through the sand bar at Lowestoft the fish had to be landed on the beach. However in the early nineteenth century, when the wind was southerly, the decked Lowestoft luggers had to anchor in North Roads, off Corton, and ferry the herring ashore here.

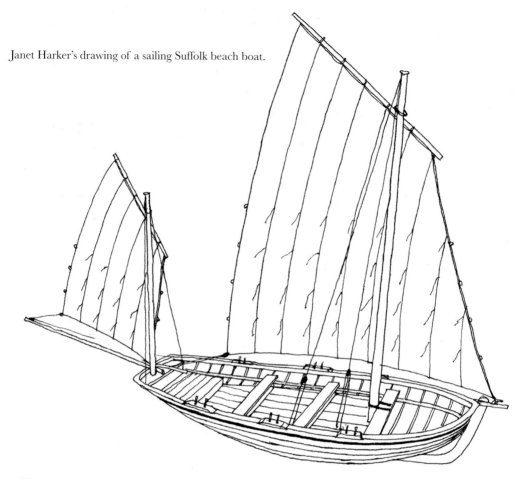

Janet Harker's drawing of a sailing Suffolk beach boat.

There were three scores at Corton, lanes leading down to the beach, where beachmen kept their boats. Between 1869 and 1879 there was a small Norfolk and Suffolk lifeboat stationed at the southernmost score. Corton had also had a small beach company.

On January 6 1905 a 'storm tide' washed a fishermen's shed and boat slipway away from the foot of Corton cliff, but Mr Colman's sea defences appear to have held. Russell Colman had erected a sea wall and groynes to protect his estate, but the heavy gales in the winter of 1907-08 seriously damaged his sea defences and he gave up the struggle because it was more than he could afford. With the sea cutting into the cliff there was nowhere for fishermen to keep their boats.

In the summer of 1910 tents were being let out at the foot of the Corton cliffs. After World War II this developed into five leisure complexes mostly with mobile homes sited on the cliff top.

Serious erosion continued but a 'Hold the Line' policy has been adopted with boulders lining the bottom of the cliff. There is a beach used by locals and people who come on holiday here. Baker's Score and Tibbenham Score, which once led down to the beachmen's landings, end abruptly at the cliff top and there are metal stairs to the beach. The gates here are locked in the winter because it is too dangerous for the public to go down on the beach.

Corton is a success story or at least, half a success story. The beachmen's landings have gone, but the village street and the five holiday complexes have been saved so far. This is one of many places where erosion has done so much damage that it is no longer possible to launch a boat regularly from the beach. Other factors in the decline of beach based fishing boats is the reduction in inshore fish stock and the mountain of regulations that the authorities have piled on fishermen. Many anglers and a few part time

This new boat is being built at Lowestoft in the International Boatbuilding Training College. This was oak on oak, based on the lines of the 15.2ft Aldeburgh sprat boat *Ossie* that had been built by Critten at Southwold in 1893.

The finished IBTC, boat on display at Maritime Woodbridge in 2014.

fishermen keep boats on open beaches, but in the spring of 2015 only one boat at Sizewell and three at Aldeburgh were regularly going to sea fishing commercially. The sea is a hard and dangerous working environment, but there are still men of courage who love the independent life and, if there were more fish out there, they would be more than willing to hunt for them.

Lowestoft Ness is the most easterly point in the British Isles. John Wylson designed the compass rose that can be seen on the ground.

# GLOSSARY

AFT. The back end or stern of a boat.

AMIDSHIPS. The area in the middle of a boat.

BEACH COMPANY. A fisherman's co-operative involved in pilotage or salvage work.

BOW. The front of a boat

CABLE. 12O fathoms, a British seafaring measurement for distance.

CARVEL. A method of building a wooden boat with planks arranged so that the sides are flat.

CLINKER BUILT. A method of building a boat, with over lapping planks.

CLOSE HAULED. The sails pulled in tight to sail close to the wind. Also called reaching when going sideways to the wind.

DENE. In Suffolk, a dene is a sandy, flat, open area near the sea and usually has some wild grasses. Often made up from eroded soil that has moved along the coast.

DOUBLE ENDED. A boat pointed at both ends.

DRIFTING. Fishing with nets hanging down from the surface while the boat drifts on the tide.

FAGGOTS. A bunch of thin tree branches bound together as a bundle large enough for one man to carry.

FATHOM. 1.8metres or 6 feet is a British measurement giving the depth of the water, or the length of a rope. This was originally the outstretched span of a man's arms, roughly six feet.

FOOT. 30.48 centimetres. British unit of measurement based on the length of a man's foot that is very convenient for stepping out lengths. Usually written as 'ft' and divided into twelve inches. There were three feet in one yard.

FLOOD TIDE. The rising tide.

FORESAIL or Fores'l. Largest sail on a lug rigged boat with two masts.

GANSEY. This is a jersey worn by seaman, or fishermen

NEAP TIDE. The small tides every two weeks when the moon is waning. In Anglo-Saxon *nep* meant 'lacking' so that neap tide became *nepflod.*

HEAD Front of a boat.

KEDGE ANCHOR. A spare anchor, smaller than the main 'bower' anchor, often used for kedging (hauling) a boat along.

LEEWARD. (or pronounced LO'WARD.) The downwind side of a boat.

LONGLINES. Winter fishing method. Individual baited hooks hang down from a line under water, between two buoys.

NESS. A Norse word for a headland, mostly used on the East Coast.

REEF. To make a sail smaller so that the boat is safe to sail in strong winds.

RNLI. The Royal National Lifeboat Institution.

ROADS. A sheltered anchorage. Usually just off the coast.

SPRING TIDE. The highest tide caused by a full moon. The highest equinoctial tides come in the spring and autumn. The Anglo-Saxon for spring tide was *fyllepflod. Fyllan* means 'to fill' while *flod* was 'to flow.' *Tyd* or tide meant 'time.'

SETT. A long pole used on yawls, lifeboats and sailing barges to push away from the shore or a quay.

STERN. The back of a boat.

TRAMMEL NET. A net under the surface that hangs down and catches fish feeding on the bottom. Can be anchored or drifting. Sometimes called 'strop gear' because it is hooked to the boat by a strop.

THOLE. A wooden peg used for a rowlock and for controlling the fishing gear when it is in the water.

THWART. A seat across an open boat that strengthens the hull.

WINDWARD. The side of a boat that the wind is coming from.

YARD. The spar at the head of a lug or square sail.

YAWL. Pronounced 'yoll' from a Norse word for a boat. A doubled ended, clinker, two masted lugger used in salvaging, pilotage or passenger work.

# Select Bibliography

Arnott, W.G. *Alde Estuary.* Ipswich 1952.

Bacon, Jean & Stuart *The Search for Dunwich City under the Sea.*1979.

Benham, Hervey *Down Tops'l.* London 1951

Benham, Hervey *The Salvagers.* Colchester 1980

Bristow, J.P. *Aldeburgh Diary.* Aldeburgh Museum 2000.

Carter, George Goldsmith *Looming Lights.* London 1945

Dickerson, Reg *Messages From the Coast.* Ipswich. 2006

Gifford, Edwin and Joyce *Anglo-Saxon Sailing Ship.* Ramsholt 1997.

Hancock, Peter *Sunk on the Sunrise Coast.* Stroud. 2008.

Higgins, David *The Beachmen.* Lavenham 1987.

Margittai, Sara & Alex Burwood *Cosy in the Winter. History of Shingle Street.* Newbury 2010.

Rose, Jack & Dean Parkin *The Grit.* Lowestoft 1997

Rouse, Michael *Coastal Resorts of East Anglia.* Lavenham, 1982

*Sea Breezes Magazine.* Volume 19, 1955.

Simper, Robert *Beach Boats of Britain.* Woodbridge 1984.

Simper, Robert *Sunrise Coast.* Ramsholt 2002

Summers, Dorothy *The East Coast Floods.* Newton Abbot 1978.

Thompson, Leonard P. *Smugglers of the Suffolk Coast.* Ipswich 1968.

Williamson, Tom *Sandlings.* Macclesfield 2005.

Winter, John *Will They Ever Learn? A history of Southwold Harbour.* Southwold 2013.

Wren, Wilfrid J. *Ports of the Eastern Counties* Lavenham 1976.

## Robert Simper

Robert Simper was born and always lived in Suffolk and has had forty books published between 1967 and 2015. In 2011 the World Ship Trust gave him an 'Individual Achievement Award in recognition of his dedication over many years to the detailed recording and documenting, both in word and photograph, of East Coast working sailing craft, and in appreciation of his own preservation activities coupled with his tireless encouragement of others.' He is a partner in Simpers of Suffolk, East Coast Fish.